Focus on U.S. History:

The Era of Colonization and Settlement

Kathy Sammis

J. WESTON
WALCH
PUBLISHER

Portland, Maine

User's Guide
to
Walch Reproducible Books

As part of our general effort to provide educational materials which are as practical and economical as possible, we have designated this publication a "reproducible book." The designation means that purchase of the book includes purchase of the right to limited reproduction of all pages on which this symbol appears:

Here is the basic Walch policy: We grant to individual purchasers of this book the right to make sufficient copies of reproducible pages for use by all students of a single teacher. This permission is limited to a single teacher, and does not apply to entire schools or school systems, so institutions purchasing the book should pass the permission on to a single teacher. Copying of the book or its parts for resale is prohibited.

Any questions regarding this policy or requests to purchase further reproduction rights should be addressed to:

Permissions Editor
J. Weston Walch, Publisher
321 Valley Street • P. O. Box 658
Portland, Maine 04104-0658

CREDITS

North Wind Picture Archives: pages 5, 8, 55, 82, 87, 91

© 1994 Corel Corporation: page 8

Dover Publications, Inc.: pages 67, 68, 80, 81, 96, 97

1   2   3   4   5   6   7   8   9   10
ISBN 0-8251-3335-1

CONTENTS

UNIT 5. SOCIAL AND CULTURAL LIFE

UNIT 6. THE COLONIAL ECONOMY

UNIT 7. THE RISE OF SLAVERY

TO THE TEACHER

The era of colonization and settlement was a profoundly transforming time for the affected areas of North America. Native American cultures and the land itself were irrevocably changed. Europeans who came to the Americas were correspondingly transformed by the new land and cultures they encountered, and by the opportunity and necessity of creating a new life and society in a new land. Conflicts between the two groups inevitably occurred as well. The colonial era also saw the introduction and spread of African slavery in the Americas, adding another new people and more cultural crosscurrents to the mix. As European settlement spread and took hold in the colonial area, new political and religious practices and institutions grew up, independent and distinct from the old-country institutions the colonists had left behind. A varied and vibrant colonial economy—actually, an aggregate of regional economies—also took hold and began to thrive.

The reproducible student activities in this book are designed to draw students into the colonial experience so they develop a rich understanding of how a basic national identity took form and a national history—whose strands run sometimes straight, sometimes winding, to today—began. Many activities in this book use original source documents to make the experiences and thoughts of people who lived centuries ago accessible to students, to show how real people viewed and affected pivotal events in their own lifetimes that are now history.

Organization

The student activity topics are divided into units guided by the National Standards for History. Each unit begins with several Student Background Pages that give the most relevant information on that unit's topic. Several reproducible student activity pages follow. They include reading selections from original contemporary sources as well as various decision-making comprehension, analytical, comparative, chronological, interpretive, research, mapping and graphing, role-playing, interactive, and interdisciplinary activities.

Each unit includes some extra challenge activities to provide enrichment for more advanced or adventurous students. Time line activities reinforce chronology, while inviting students into broader descriptive and illustrative areas. Two maps are provided, for use in several units; you may make copies as needed. The map of Colonial North America is used in Units 1, 2, and 6. The map of the Atlantic region is used in Units 4, 6, and 7.

Each unit is preceded by a teacher guide that gives you an overview of the unit and its objectives, plus specific teaching suggestions for each student activity.

The original source quotations are presented with modern spelling, modern capitalization, and modernized punctuation. The colonial style of writing favored lengthy sentences and formal vocabulary. Where appropriate, we have punctuated to shorten sentences and added explanations of archaic words. Still, it is important that these selections sound like the colonial people who wrote them. So in the teacher's guide to each unit, we've suggested that you might want to go over the original source selections in class, to be sure all students understand the vocabulary being used and the colonial syntax.

At the back of this book is a section titled Answer Key, Additional Activities, Assessments, with answers for all student activities, suggested additional activities, and an assessment vehicle for each unit. The resource section lists fiction and nonfiction books plus electronic and other resources for research and enrichment. The glossary is reproducible for student use.

TO THE STUDENT

During the 1600's and 1700's, the nation we now call the United States began to take shape. Until that time, the land was inhabited only by Native Americans. Then, Europeans began arriving. They came in a trickle at first, which grew into a steady stream. Some came of their own free will. Some came because they were forced to, as convicts or bound servants. Africans came too, in increasing numbers. Sadly, they came against their will, forced into slavery to provide labor for colonial businesses, especially southern plantations.

As these people met and mingled, a new society and culture began to emerge. Ignoring European class systems, independent-minded American colonists insisted on a big voice in running things. They set up new ways of governing themselves. They set standards in law and in practice for religious freedom. They also developed a thriving economy.

In the process, though, Native Americans lost their lands and their lives. Africans lost their homeland, their culture, and their freedom.

The activities you'll be doing for this course of study will help you better understand this era of colonizing and settling. You'll work with maps and graphs. You'll put yourself into the shoes of colonial people, deciding whether you can vote, choosing a business to start up, debating whether to enter into a fur-trading enterprise with Europeans. You'll read what colonial people themselves had to say about their lives. You'll also read some original charters and laws whose provisions still apply to your life today. When you're finished, you'll have a better grasp of how the United States was shaped during this very important colonial period. You'll see what kind of a vibrant mix was poised on the brink of revolution by the 1760's.

           Focus on U.S. History:
The Era of Colonization and Settlement

Name _____   Date _____

Map of Colonial North America

for use with Units 1, 2, and 6

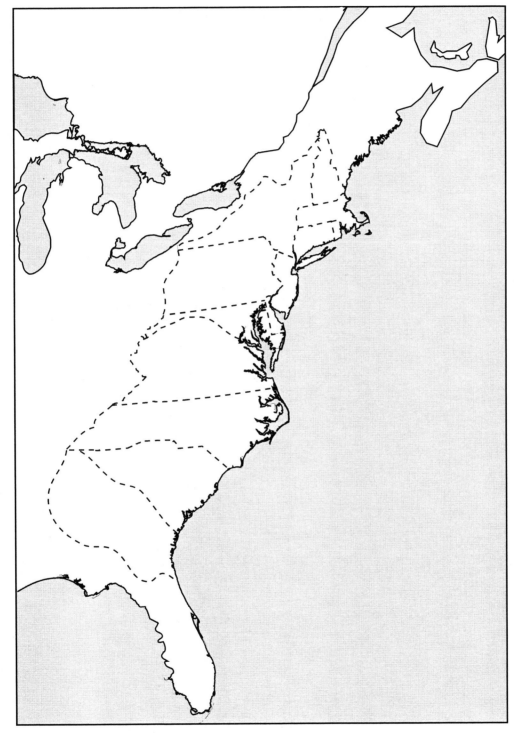

Focus on U.S. History:
The Era of Colonization and Settlement

Name _____ Date _____

Map of the Atlantic Region

for use with Units 4, 6, and 7

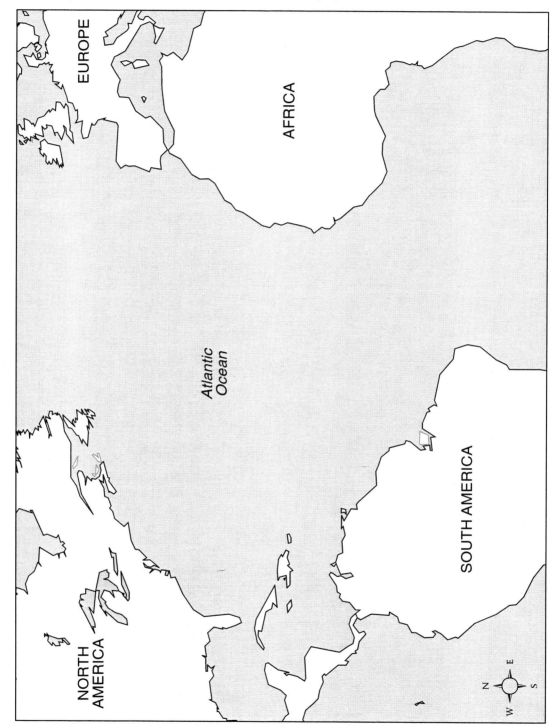

Focus on U.S. History:
The Era of Colonization and Settlement

The Early Colonists

The objective of this unit is to give students an understanding of how European immigrants from various backgrounds helped form the North American colonies. The decision to emigrate (for those who had a choice in the matter) was not made lightly. The sea voyage was long, difficult, uncomfortable, expensive, and dangerous. The North American settlements were young; life in frontier areas was primitive. Some immigrants were forced to come—by the justice system or by economic necessity. (We examine the forced emigration of Africans into slavery in Unit 7.) Others came for religious or political reasons, for adventure, or for profit. The activities in this unit help students understand all these aspects of colonial immigration.

Student Activities

The student background pages include an extra challenge activity. Students put themselves into the place of colonial promoters. They use what they have learned about why people might emigrate and how colonial immigration was promoted to create a "COME TO . . ." handbill for their colony. This would be a good wrap-up activity for the unit.

Mapping the Spread of European Settlements on the map of colonial North America shows how waves of European immigration spread settlements up and down colonial North America. Students finish up by creating a settlement time line from the dates they have identified.

Graphing European Immigration and **Reading the Immigration Pie Charts** show the ethnic composition of various colonies, underlining the diversity of the middle colonies and the primarily English or British nature of New England and the southern colonies.

Wanted: Colonists is the first of several original-source documents included in this book's student activities. You might want to go over these aloud in class to assure that all students understand them.

Would You Emigrate? draws on the **Wanted: Colonists** readings and the student background pages. Students put themselves in the place of potential European emigrants and identify why they might make a decision to emigrate. (Unit 4 examines religious reasons for making such a decision if students need help with these.) In the extra challenge activity students role-play discussing an emigration decision.

Those Who Came to the Colonies describes actual emigrants. Students use these descriptions to identify specific groups who came to the colonies: transported convicts, indentured servants, orphans, and so on. The extra reading selection gives students a flavor of the scary and very unpleasant possibilities of a transatlantic voyage.

Come to the Colonies! shows how not everything that people believed and hoped of the North American colonies was true. Students identify the inaccuracies in various promotional descriptions. *Caveat emptor.*

A Tale of Two Colonies uses summary descriptions and a comparison chart to help students identify why British North America's first two permanent settlements very nearly had quite different outcomes—why Plymouth flourished almost at once, and why Jamestown almost failed.

The Early Colonists

From the late 1400's through the 1500's, Europeans busily explored the "New World" that they had finally discovered. In the 1600's the European Age of Discovery gave way to an age of colonizing and settling. (We'll look at the conflicts this created, especially with Native Americans, in Unit 2.) Four major European powers competed for a share of North America: the Dutch, the French, the Spanish, and the English.

The **Spanish** established some settlements in North America very early—St. Augustine (Florida) in 1576 and Santa Fe (New Mexico) in 1610, for example. However, Spain focused most of its colonizing efforts farther south, in Central and South America and the Caribbean islands.

The **Dutch** started trading for furs with the Indians on the Hudson River in 1609. They founded New Amsterdam (later New York City) in 1624. Dutch settlers spread out a bit from this settlement over the next 50 years. However, the focus of Dutch interest in North America was on trade, not on settling large numbers of colonists. The Dutch colony of New Netherland fell to the English in 1664 and became New York.

Like the Dutch, the **French** were most interested in the North American fur trade. Exchanging goods for furs with Native Americans didn't call for large settlements. The French simply set up strings of small, isolated trading posts in northern areas. French Jesuit priests came and lived among Indians they hoped to convert to the Catholic faith. Some French settlers eventually came and founded scattered towns. However, they were greatly outnumbered by settlers in the English colonies to the south.

From the outset, the **English** intended to fill their North American colonies with settlers. The early explorers had found a vast land rich in natural resources. Spreading settlers over this land would give England, not some other European nation, control of its potential wealth. Wealthy upper-class Englishmen got charters from their government to establish colonies.

(continued)

The Early Colonists *(continued)*

Why They Came

However, the streams of settlers who flowed across the Atlantic Ocean in the late 1600's and 1700's weren't members of the nobility. They were country gentry, merchants, yeoman farmers, and artisan-shopkeepers—in part. Many more were poor people, at the bottom of the social and economic ladder. Some were criminals and vagrants. The British government saved itself the cost of keeping them in jail by sending them off to the colonies. Others were *indentured servants*. These men and women sold themselves to a master for a given number of years. In return, the master paid for the servant's trip and living expenses. Sometimes people were kidnapped and sold as servants against their will. Conditions aboard ships on the way over were often horrible. Masters could be harsh, bent on wringing every possible ounce of labor out of servants during their terms.

Why were so many thousands upon thousands of people willing to sell themselves into virtual slavery for several years? Because the opportunities for poor people in the colonies simply did not exist for poor people in Europe. These prospects also lured other colonists. Land to own and farm was scarce in England and other countries. In families lucky enough to own land, the entire estate usually passed to the oldest son. Younger sons had to look elsewhere for a living. Land was abundant in the colonies. All sorts of businesses were needed and could thrive. Free emigrants could start right away to build their new lives. Once their term of service was over, transported convicts and indentured servants could pursue whatever calling appealed to them. Sometimes they got a

grant of land and start-up farming equipment at the end of their contract.

Colonists came to North America for religious reasons as well. You'll read about this in Unit 4.

Political conflicts also created colonists. For example, when King Charles I was beheaded, in 1649, Oliver Cromwell ruled England. Royal supporters who opposed Cromwell fled to the colonies. After Cromwell died, in 1658, Charles II took the English throne. Now, Cromwell's backers left for the colonies. Scots who rebelled against the British king in 1745 were pardoned if they moved to America.

This land of opportunity appealed to many. New England was settled mostly by English and Scottish colonists. Other colonies had more diverse populations. New York and parts of New Jersey and Delaware had begun as New Netherland, so they had many Dutch settlers. Pennsylvania attracted large numbers of Germans looking for religious freedom. Scots who had taken over Northern Ireland felt oppressed by their English rulers. These "Scotch-Irish" poured into the colonies. Fiercely independent, they populated much of western Pennsylvania and the Virginia and Carolina backcountry.

One group of colonists, of course, did not come willingly: black Africans, sent to the colonies as slaves. You'll read about this sad aspect of colonization in Unit 7.

(continued)

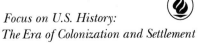

Focus on U.S. History:
The Era of Colonization and Settlement

The Early Colonists *(continued)*

Extra Challenge

Imagine you and a group of friends have gotten a charter to set up a new colony in North America. You hope to make a lot of money on this venture.

To succeed, your colony needs settlers. Use what you learn in this unit about the colonies and early colonists to create an advertisement or poster intended to persuade people to emigrate to your colony and settle there. Your ad should be eye-catching and exciting and promise great things—but it should also be reasonably accurate.

Mapping the Spread of European Settlements

Directions: Locate and label each of these colonies and towns on the map of Colonial North America. Add the date each was founded. Also, show whether it was French, Dutch, English, Spanish, or Swedish. (Hint: The colonies and towns are listed in the order in which they were founded, from the earliest date to the latest.)

St. Augustine

Roanoke

Port Royal, Nova Scotia

Jamestown

Quebec

Fort Nassau (Albany)

Plymouth

New Amsterdam (New York)

Boston, Massachusetts Bay Colony

St. Mary's, Maryland Colony

Providence

Hartford

Fort Christiana, New Sweden

New Haven

New London

New Jersey Colony

Charles Town, South Carolina

New Hampshire Colony

Philadelphia, Pennsylvania Colony

Germantown, Pennsylvania

Delaware (separate assembly established)

New Orleans

Baltimore

Georgia Colony

Challenge Question:

What common geographic feature do most of these early towns share?

Time Line: Use the founding dates on your map to create a time line of the spread of settlements in colonial North America.

Settlers setting up camp

5

Focus on U.S. History:
The Era of Colonization and Settlement

Graphing European Immigration

The first U.S. Census, taken in 1790, showed the European origins of the white U.S. population for each state/colony. Look at these pie charts for some representative states/colonies.

U.S. Population at First Census, 1790

Massachusetts
(a New England colony)

English	82%
Scotch	4.4%
Irish	3.9%
German	0.3%
Dutch	0.2%
French	0.8%
Unclassified	8.4%

New York
(a middle colony)

English	52%
Dutch	17.5%
German	8.2%
Scotch	7%
Irish	8.1%
French	3.8%
Swedish	0.5%
Unclassified	2.9%

Pennsylvania
(a middle colony)

English	35.3%
German	33.3%
Irish	14.5%
Scotch	8.6%
Dutch	1.8%
French	1.8%
Swedish	0.8%
Unclassified	3.9%

South Carolina
(a southern colony)

English	60.2%
Scotch	15%
Irish	13.8%
German	5%
Dutch	0.4%
French	3.9%
Swedish	0.2%
Unclassified	1.5%

Reading the Immigration Pie Charts

Directions: Learn more about the white immigrant population of the British North American colonies by answering these questions. Use the information in the immigration pie charts.

1. In which colonies were most people of English origin?

   _____

2. In which colonies were about 90 percent of the people from Great Britain and Ireland?

   _____

3. Which colony had the most ethnically diverse population? _____

   _____

   Why might this have been true? _____

   _____

4. What ethnic group made up nearly 20 percent of New York's population? _____

   _____

   Why would this have been so? _____

5. In which colony did people originally from Germany make up over one quarter of the population?

   _____

6. What were the two second-largest ethnic groups in South Carolina? _____

   _____

Extra Challenge:

From the pie chart information, develop a general statement about each type of colony's population.

   (a) New England: _____

   (b) Middle colonies: _____

   (c) Southern colonies: _____

Focus on U.S. History:
The Era of Colonization and Settlement

Wanted: Colonists

Promoters, religious leaders, and others offered a variety of reasons for colonizing North America. Here are some, in their own words.

William Bradford, Pilgrim leader (early 1600's)

[On why the Pilgrims left England:] The work of God was no sooner manifest in them, but presently they were both scoffed and scorned by the profane multitude. . . . They could not long continue in any peaceable condition, but were hunted and persecuted on every side, so as their former afflictions were but as flea-bitings in comparison of these which now came upon them.

Sir George Peckham, investor in colonizing ventures (1583)

[T]he trade, traffic, and planting in those countries is likely to prove very profitable to the whole realm in general [and] to the particular profit of all adventurers. . . . And in the whole tract of that land [is] great plenty of mineral matter of all sorts, and in very many places, . . . and great stores of beasts, birds, and fowls both for pleasure and necessary use of man are to be found.

William Symonds, London minister (1609)

The reason why God will have His to fill the earth is because the Lord would have His works to be known . . . . [O]ne that hath the knowledge of the fear of God should communicate it to others . . . [T]he Lord . . . doth . . . call you to go and carry the Gospel to a nation that never heard of Christ.

The people, blessed be God, do swarm in the land [England] as young bees in a hive in June; insomuch that there is very hardly room for one man to live by another. . . . Lords of manors convert townships, in which were a hundred or two hundred communicants, to a shepherd and his dog. The true laboring husbandman . . . is now in many places turned laborer, and can hardly escape the statute of rogues and vagrants.

General James Oglethorpe, founder of Georgia colony (1733)

In America there are fertile lands sufficient to subsist all the useless poor in England, and distressed Protestants in Europe. [In this colony] many families, who would otherwise starve, will be provided for, and made masters of houses and lands. The people in Great Britain to whom these needy families were a burden, will be relieved. Numbers of manufacturers will here [in England] be employed for supplying them with clothes, working tools, and other necessaries. And by giving refuge to the distressed Salzburgers and other persecuted Protestants, the power of Britain, as a reward for its hospitality, will be increased by the addition of so many religious and industrious subjects.

Focus on U.S. History:
The Era of Colonization and Settlement

Name _____

Date _____

Would You Emigrate?

Directions: Would you leave your native country to settle in a new, unknown (perhaps even a frontier) colony? This is a big decision! Imagine you are each of the people described here. Use what you have read to tell why you might (or might not) decide to emigrate to North America.

1. You are a recently ordained minister in Germany. You believe all people would benefit from embracing the Christian religion. Why might you choose to emigrate?

2. You fought for Bonnie Prince Charlie at the Battle of Culloden in Scotland, in 1746. Why might you choose to emigrate?

3. You are an unmarried Irish woman, age 20, living in a small village with your parents. Why might you choose to emigrate?

4. You are an English Puritan who strongly objects to the rituals of the Anglican Church (the Church of England). Why might you choose to emigrate?

5. You are a Huguenot (Protestant) in overwhelmingly Catholic France. Why might you choose to emigrate?

6. You have been a loyal supporter of the king of England. Now it is 1653, and Oliver Cromwell is ruling England. Why might you choose to emigrate?

7. For generations, your family has been tenant farmers in England. Now the lord who owns the land that you farm is converting to sheep raising. Why might you choose to emigrate?

8. You are a Dutch merchant. Why might you choose to emigrate?

9. You are the younger son of an English nobleman. Why might you choose to emigrate?

Extra Challenge:
Team up with one or several classmates. Role-play, discussing your thoughts about emigrating with neighbor(s) and relative(s).

9

Focus on U.S. History:
The Era of Colonization and Settlement

Those Who Came to the Colonies

Directions: Here are some descriptions of real people who sailed from England to the Americas in the 1600's.* Read them. Then use what you've read to list various types of people who were North America's early colonists.

1613 John Gerarde, citizen and barber surgeon of London, adventurer in Virginia

1614 Henry Bourne of Edgware, yeoman, and William Clarke of Edgware, convicted of stealing sheep; respited for transportation to the Bermudas

1614 Joan Sansom of Whitechapel, spinster, found not guilty of stealing but ordered to be sent to the Bermudas

1617 Stephen Rogers, convicted of a killing and reprieved, ordered to be sent to Virginia because he is a carpenter

1618 Ralph Rooke, an incorrigible rogue and vagabond, sentenced to be transported to Virginia

1618 William Makepeace, brought in as a vagrant boy and young rogue, to be kept at work until he is sent to Virginia

1620 Ellen Boulter, brought in for a vagrant that will not be ruled by her father or her friends, to be kept at her father's charge and sent to Virginia

1621 Thomas Markham, a lewd boy that will not be ruled by his parents but continually cometh away, to be sent to Virginia

1629 Sir William Alexander, [commissioned] to voyage to the Gulf of Canada to trade for furs and skins

1634 Mr. Ward of Ipswich has preached against the Book of Common Prayer thus causing this giddiness and desire to go to New England

*Adapted from *The Complete Book of Emigrants, 1607–1660,* compiled by Peter Wilson Coldham (Baltimore, MD: Genealogical Publishing Co., 1987.
© 1987 by Peter Wilson Coldham. All Rights Reserved.

(continued)

Those Who Came to the Colonies *(continued)*

1634 The Providence Island Company: Women are to be sent over as servants to provide wives for planters

1653 Henry Chillman, of Finchley, Middlesex, took possession of the property of Jeremy Littleboy, of Finchley, on his death in about 1628. So that the son Lawrence Littleboy should not inherit, Chillman packed him off to Virginia when he was still a minor.

1653 License to Richard Netherway, of Bristol, to transport 100 Irish Tories from Ireland to Virginia

1653 Order for Bartholomew Broome, aged 11, who was stolen and put on board a ship bound for Virginia to be restored to his father Robert Broome

1654 Thomas, son of Thomas Ree, of Upper Warren, Worcs., yeoman, bound to William Willett, of Bristol, merchant, to serve six years in Virginia

1655 Katherine Mathew, of Swansea, Glamorgan, spinster, bound to William Boddy of Virginia, planter, to serve 6 years in Virginia and to receive 50 acres

1655 Christian Chacrett, alias Sacrett, and Thomas Orpitt, alias Allpitt, summoned to answer for taking up men, women and children and selling them to be sent overseas

Types of Early Colonists:

_____   _____

_____   _____

_____   _____

_____   _____

_____   _____

_____   _____

(continued)

Focus on U.S. History:
The Era of Colonization and Settlement

Those Who Came to the Colonies *(continued)*

The voyage across the Atlantic could be terrifying, and very unpleasant. Here are two accounts of trips, one in 1629 and the other 1679.

Reverend Francis Higginson (1629):

Wednesday the wind [was] still north and calm in the morning. But about noon there arose a south wind, which increased more and more, so that it proved to us that are landmen a sore and terrible storm. For the wind blew mightily, the rain fell vehemently, the sea roared and the waves tossed us horribly. Besides, it was fearful dark and the mariner's mate was afraid. . . . The waves poured themselves over the ship [so] that the two [life] boats were filled with water.

Jaspar Dankers and Peter Sluyter (1679):

The passengers and crew were a wretched set. There was no rest, night or day, especially among the wives—a rabble I cannot describe. It was as if they were in the fish market or apple market, night and day, without cessation. . . . Among the men there were some persons who drank like beasts, yes, drank themselves dead drunk, as you may judge from the fact that two or three of them drank thirty-five gallons of brandy, besides wine, from the time we left England or Holland. *In fine*, it was a Babel. I have never in my life heard of such a disorderly ship. It was confusion without end. I have never been in a ship where there was so much vermin. . . . There were some bunks and clothes as full as if they had been sown.

How would you have enjoyed being on a long voyage aboard either of these ships?

Focus on U.S. History:
The Era of Colonization and Settlement

Come to the Colonies!

Directions: The people promoting the colonies didn't always have an accurate notion of what settlers and traders would find there. Read these promotional descriptions. Then tell what is **inaccurate** about each one.

Sir George Peckham, investor in colonies (1583)

It is well known that all savages, . . . so soon as they shall begin but a little to taste of civility, will take marvelous delight in any garment, be it never so simple—as a shirt, a blue, yellow, red, or green cotton cassock, a cap, or such like—and will take incredible pains for such a trifle. . . . Which being so, what vent for our English clothes will thereby ensue, and how great benefit to all such persons [who are involved in manufacturing clothing in England].

1. What is inaccurate about this? _____

_____

Neither may I here omit the great hope and likelihood of a passage beyond the Grand Bay into the South Seas, confirmed by sundry authors, to be found leading to Cathay, the Moluccas and the Spice Islands.

2. What is inaccurate about this? _____

_____

It is not to be forgotten, what trifles they be that the savages do require in exchange of these commodities: yea, for pearls, gold, silver, and precious stones.

3. What is inaccurate about this? _____

_____

General James Oglethorpe, founder of Georgia Colony (1733)

The colony of Georgia lying about the same latitude with part of China, Persia, Palestine, and the Madeiras, it is highly probable that when it shall be well-peopled and rightly cultivated, England may be supplied from thence with raw silk, wine, oil, dyes, drugs, and many other materials . . . which she is obliged to purchase from southern countries.

4. What is inaccurate about this? _____

_____

First Charter of Virginia (1606)

We do grant and agree, . . . that the said several colonies shall and lawfully may give and take order to dig, mine, and search for all manner of mines of gold, silver, and copper; yielding to us the fifth part only of all the same gold and silver so to be gotten or had.

5. What is unrealistic about this? _____

_____

13   *Focus on U.S. History:*
The Era of Colonization and Settlement

A Tale of Two Colonies

Read these two descriptions of the founding of the first two permanent British settlements in North America.

Jamestown

Most of the Jamestown colonists were gentlemen and gentlemen's servants. English gentlemen and their servants never performed manual labor. They were no more prepared to do so in America than in their native land. The gentlemen came to Virginia expecting to find lots of gold and silver. They planned to spend their time gathering these precious metals, or perhaps overseeing as their servants did the gathering. When they found they had to work hard, they began quarreling among themselves.

Nongentlemen settlers were hired workers. They were working for the colonizing company, not for themselves. They had no incentive to work hard, so they didn't. The Jamestown leaders—appointed by the colonizing company—weren't very skilled, so they couldn't stop the conflict or get people to work harder.

The Jamestown colonists chose the site of their settlement because it was on the river. They thought they could defend it easily against Indian attack. In fact, the land was swampy, and the drinking water wasn't good. In this climate, many settlers died of malaria and dysentery. Their relations with the Native Americans weren't smooth. In fact, attacks were always a possibility.

During the summer, the colonists didn't catch and salt extra fish to eat over the winter. They didn't get enough crops grown and harvested, either. During the winter of 1608–1609, the Jamestown settlers suffered through the "Starving Time." Many died. One man even killed his wife, salted her body to preserve it, and began eating her! (He was caught at it and executed.) Finally, John Smith took control of the colony. He bought corn from the Native Americans. He got the colonists to be orderly and practical.

Plymouth

The Plymouth settlers came to America so they could practice their religion in the way they wanted. They were not gentry. They knew they were coming to a near-wilderness without riches like gold or silver. They came to work hard to create a new, holy society that would follow God's word in all things. Before landing in America, the male settlers signed an agreement. They promised to live by a set of rules they themselves would draw up. And they did. They also chose their own leaders.

The Pilgrims landed in December, so they couldn't grow food until the following summer. Many died that winter of starvation. But their site had plenty of fresh air and water. They made sure their relations with nearby Native Americans were friendly. One man in particular, Squanto, showed them how to grow corn. The Pilgrims had plenty of food on hand when their second winter began.

(continued)

*Focus on U.S. History:
The Era of Colonization and Settlement*

A Tale of Two Colonies *(continued)*

Directions: The Jamestown colony almost failed in its earliest years. The Plymouth colony established itself strongly during its first year (after the first, starving winter). Use the chart below to identify why the two colonies had such different experiences.

	Jamestown	**Plymouth**
Site		
The Colonists Themselves		
How Colony Was Governed		
Relations with Native Americans		
Reasons for Coming to Colony		
Food Supply		

Focus on U.S. History:
The Era of Colonization and Settlement

Colonial Conflicts and Native Americans

The objective of this unit is to help students understand the conflicts created as European colonizers struggled for control of North America and the resulting interactions between Europeans and Native Americans. The different colonial powers and their settlers evolved different relationships with Indians. These interactions affected both white and Native American cultures, as well as relations among various tribal groups. Rivalries among the European nations caused violence on the colonial frontier and involved Indian societies in the conflicts. Inevitably, the Europeans' desire for permanent settlement and land ownership led to conflict with native inhabitants. This unit's activities will lead to better understanding of these aspects of colonization and settlement.

Student Activities

French and British Wars briefly describes the four major European wars that spilled over into the colonies. Students identify the French and British losses and gains at the end of each war, some of which seem quite insubstantial compared with the loss of life.

Mutual Influences—The Columbian Exchange offers a way to compare how Native Americans and Europeans absorbed specific aspects of each other's culture.

European Views of Native Americans consists of original-source quotes. (Again, you may want to review these pieces in class to be sure all students understand them.)

In **Living Together: Europeans and Native Americans**, students connect the European views they have just read with actual outcomes by predicting what kind of relations occurred between Native Americans and Europeans in three colonies. Students then test the validity of their predictions by checking references to see what actually happened.

Enemies and Allies gives students an idea of the number of violent conflicts and changing alliances between colonists and native tribes. As an extension of this activity, you could assign individuals or groups to write descriptions of each conflict and its outcome. In the extra challenge activity, students locate the areas where each conflict took place on their map of Colonial North America from Unit 1.

Close-up: The Fur Trade gives a detailed look at how this important element of European-Indian interaction affected Native Americans. After reading the close-up, students identify environmental, social, and economic effects fur trading had on the Native American societies. The extra challenge activity asks students to find a modern example of a sudden new demand for a resource that has had comparable wide-ranging effects.

Time Line: Indian and Colonial Wars has students identify dates of these violent clashes and add them to their time line. Brief descriptions and illustrations enrich this activity.

Two Native American Views presents two possible reactions to the European invasion: fight or give way. Students examine both alternatives in small groups and put themselves in the place of Native Americans trying to make the difficult decision of what to do.

Name _____

Date _____

Colonial Conflicts and Native Americans

As you learned in Unit 1, the Dutch, the Spanish, the French, and the British all played an active role in colonizing North America. These European powers clashed with one another. They also interacted both peacefully and violently with the Native Americans they encountered.

The **French** interest in North America focused primarily on the hugely profitable fur trade. This meant leaving tribal lands undisturbed so Native Americans could roam them freely, trapping and piling up furs. Trappers would bring the pelts to small, scattered French trading posts in northern North America. There they would exchange their furs for goods. Both sides seemed to benefit from this exchange, and it was in the French interest to cultivate good relations with their Native American trading partners. So French-Indian interactions were generally quite friendly.

Native American and European Views of Land

Europeans believed in private land ownership by individuals. They said they could claim any "unsettled" or "unimproved" land.

Native Americans believed that the land was a gift from the Creator. The land was to be shared and used by all living creatures for their mutual benefit.

Can you see how these two views would cause problems when Europeans started arriving in lands where Native Americans lived?

Dutch relations with Native Americans were of two types. The Dutch had started trading for furs with the Indians in 1609, during Henry Hudson's exploring trip. The Dutch set up a small trading post near Albany in 1614. New Amsterdam, founded in 1621, was also a fur trading center. As long as the Dutch were primarily engaged in the fur trade, they worked hard to stay friendly with the Native Americans, as the French did.

However, after 1635 Dutch settlers began spreading out on Indian land around New Amsterdam. Typical conflicts followed. Dutch forces wiped out Raritans in 1641, on Staten Island. In 1643 Dutch soldiers massacred a peaceful group of Wecquaesgeeks who were camped, with Dutch leaders' approval, around New Amsterdam. After the British captured New Amsterdam, in 1664, the Dutch no longer controlled relations with Indians in that area.

Spanish interactions with Native Americans in the colonizing years were limited mainly to the Southwest and Florida. After the Spanish explorers and conquistadors came Franciscan friars. These priests established a series of mission settlements among Pueblo Indians of the Southwest and among Native American tribes of northern Florida and nearby coastal regions. Their purpose was to convert the Indians to Christianity. Their method was to use the natives as forced labor. Indians built the missions, grew the crops, and performed all the work in the settlements.

(continued)

Colonial Conflicts and Native Americans *(continued)*

In 1680 a religious leader named Popé led the Pueblos in an uprising that drove the Spanish out of Santa Fe and New Mexico. The Spanish didn't regain control of that area until 1692. The Florida settlements were destroyed by the late 1600's, falling both to English settlers in the Carolinas and to the Native Americans themselves.

Most of Colonial North America was taken over by **British** settlers. So, interactions with the British had the greatest impact on Native Americans. Unlike the French and Dutch fur traders or the Spanish friars, English colonists came to live on the land. They created settlements, villages, towns, farms, plantations. They cleared forests to plant crops. They fenced off pastures for their livestock. Time and again, this led to conflicts between the European settlers and the Native Americans whose land was being settled. Even when relations began on a friendly basis, they usually ended violently.

In Massachusetts, English-speaking Indians showed the Pilgrims where to catch fish and how to grow corn. Native Americans and colonists celebrated the first Thanksgiving together in 1621. By 1675 these same groups were at war with each other. In Virginia, Captain John Smith established peace with the chief Powhatan soon after Jamestown was founded in 1607. In 1622 the chief's brother Opechancanough led a massacre of the Jamestown settlers.

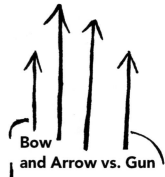

Bow and Arrow vs. Gun

Today's guns are much more accurate than a bow and arrow. But seventeenth-century muskets were not! And they were very heavy. You could hit a moving target much more easily with a bow and arrow. You could also fire off up to six arrows in the time it took to reload a musket.

William Penn and Roger Williams made friendly relations with Indians one of the founding concepts for their colonies, Pennsylvania and Rhode Island. Both Penn and Williams paid Native Americans for their land and insisted that they be treated fairly. But in Pennsylvania, as in Virginia, the Carolinas, and Georgia, settlers kept pushing into the western frontiers. As they did, they forced the native inhabitants back and wiped them out.

In spite of many conflicts, European and Native American interaction resulted in more than violence. Europeans adopted Indian names for the new creatures and plants they found in North America. They learned how and where to find, catch, and grow American foods. They adopted practical Native American uses of animal skins for clothing—deerskin leggings and moccasins, for example. The Indian strategy of guerrilla warfare would be very effective when the colonists began fighting the British Army in the Revolutionary War.

From the Europeans, Native Americans gained useful metal tools and woolen blankets. They also acquired guns, which raised the violence level and death rate of intertribal wars. Alcohol was a deadly addition to Native American culture. Deadliest of all, though, were European diseases. American Indians had little resistance to such "new" illnesses as smallpox, measles, and chickenpox. Millions upon millions died.

Focus on U.S. History:
The Era of Colonization and Settlement

French and British Wars

During the late 1600's and 1700's, France and England fought many wars in Europe. These conflicts spilled over into North America, which both nations wanted to control. Each war had one name in Europe and another name in North America. In America, the French enlisted their Indian allies, chiefly the Algonquins, to fight against English settlers. The English got their allies, mainly the Iroquois, to fight against the French. These conflicts made life on the colonial frontiers very risky.

Directions: Read the brief descriptions below of action in each war. Then tell what the French and British losses and gains were for each.

1. **King William's War (1689–1697)** (In Europe: War of the League of Augsburg): The French and their Indian allies raid Schenectady, New York, and frontier settlements in New England. The English capture Port Royal, Nova Scotia, but then lose it.

   French gains/losses at end: _____

   British gains/losses at end: _____

2. **Queen Anne's War (1702–1713)** (In Europe: War of the Spanish Succession): The French incite their Abenaki allies to attack and destroy Deerfield, Massachusetts. English settlers from the Carolinas burn Spanish St. Augustine, Florida. New England settlers retake Port Royal.

   French gains/losses at end: _____

   British gains/losses at end: _____

3. **King George's War (1740–1748)** (In Europe: War of the Austrian Succession): New Englanders capture Louisburg, on Cape Breton Island. Many Indian raids are conducted on both sides of the frontier.

   French gains/losses at end: _____

   British gains/losses at end: _____

4. **French and Indian War (1754–1763)** (In Europe: Seven Years' War, 1756–1763): The final war, with much action on all sides. See the Time Line listing on page 25 for the major events of this war.

   French gains/losses at end: _____

   British gains/losses at end: _____

Pontiac's War

The Indians lost a powerful ally when France gave up its role in North America. Traders, settlers, and English soldiers wanted to take over Indian lands in the Ohio Valley. In 1763, Pontiac, an Ottawa chief, led a powerful alliance that tried to push the invaders back across the Allegheny Mountains. The effort failed.

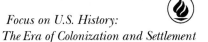

Mutual Influences—the Columbian Exchange

Directions: Contact between Europeans and Native Americans affected both peoples. Historians call this the Columbian Exchange. Below, identify specific aspects of each other's cultures that the two groups absorbed.

Native Americans
(what their culture absorbed
from European culture)

Europeans
(what their culture absorbed
from Indian culture)

Native Americans		Europeans
	language	
	clothing and coverings	
	farming	
	health	
	weapons and warfare	
	food and drink	
	commerce and ways to travel	
	tools	

Focus on U.S. History:
The Era of Colonization and Settlement

European Views of Native Americans

Different European colonists and explorers had different views about Native Americans. Some had definite opinions even though they'd never met any Indians! Read what these leaders had to say about the original North Americans.

William Penn, Pennsylvania Colony

I have made seven purchases [of land], and in pay and presents they have had at least twelve hundred pounds of me. They have some great men amongst them, I mean for wisdom, truth and justice. They speak little, but fervently, and with elegance. I have never seen more natural sagacity. . . . [H]e will deserve the name of wise who outwits them in any treaty about a thing they understand.

Edward Winslow, Plymouth Colony

We have found the Indians very faithful in their covenant of peace with us, very loving, and ready to pleasure us. We often go to them, and they come to us. Yea, it hath pleased God so to possess the Indians with a fear of us and love unto us, that . . . all the peoples round about us have . . . been glad of any occasion to make peace with us. They are a people without any religion or knowledge of any God, yet very trusty, quick of apprehension, ripe-witted, just.

William Bradford, Plymouth Colony

The place [the Pilgrims] had thoughts [of colonizing] was some of those vast and unpeopled countries of America, which are fruitful and fit for habitation, being devoid of all civil inhabitants—where there are only savage and brutish men, which range up and down, little otherwise than the wild beasts.

John Smith, Jamestown Colony

[S]ome are of disposition fearful, some bold, most cautious, all *savage*. . . . They are very strong, of an able body and full of agility, able to endure to lie in the woods by the fire in the worst of winter, or in the weeds and grass, in ambush in the summer. Let us with all speed [choose] the best seats of the county . . . by vanquishing the savages.

Anonymous Jamestown colonist

We never perceived that the natives of the country did voluntarily yield themselves subjects to our gracious sovereign [the king of England], neither that they took any pride in that title. . . . [N]or could we at any time keep them in such good respect of correspondency as we became mutually helpful each to other. Contrarily, what at any [time] was done proceeded from fear and not love, and their corn [we] procured by trade or the sword.

Living Together: Europeans and Native Americans

Directions: You have just read some views various colonists had of the Native Americans among whom they were now living. Use these views to predict what relations between Europeans and Indians were like in the early colonies listed below. Then check history references to see if your predictions are correct.

Massachusetts (Plymouth and Massachusetts Bay colonies)—
relations between Europeans and Native Americans in the 1600's:

- Your prediction:

- Actual events:

Pennsylvania—relations between Europeans and Native Americans:

- Your prediction:

- Actual events:

Virginia—relations between Europeans and Native Americans in the 1600's:

- Your prediction:

- Actual events:

Native American Place-Names

Colonists kept many Native American place-names, usually in an adapted form. Which of the 13 original colonies had Indian names? Write them here:

Challenge Question: Why did early European colonists find so many fewer Native Americans in New England than in colonies farther south?

Focus on U.S. History:
The Era of Colonization and Settlement

Enemies and Allies

Directions: All through the colonial period, European colonists and Native Americans met, interacted—and inevitably fought. Europeans wanted to own and settle the land. Indians wanted to use the same land freely. This conflict grew violent, over and over again. Identify which Native American group was involved in each conflict below. Write a correct group name in each blank. (You will use two group names twice.)

Conflicts

Jamestown Massacre (1622)

_____ vs. English colonists

Pequot War (1637)

_____ vs. English colonists and their allies:

_____ and _____

King Philip's War (1675–76)

_____ and _____ vs. English colonists

Pueblo Uprising (1680)

_____ and _____ vs. Spanish colonists

Tuscarora War (1711–13)

_____ and English colonists vs. _____

Yamasee War (1715)

_____ vs. English colonists and _____

French and Indian War (1754–1763)

English colonists and _____ vs. French colonists and _____

and _____

Pontiac's War (1763)

_____ vs. British colonists

Native American Groups
Apache
Cherokee
Delaware
Hurons
Iroquois
Mohicans
Narragansetts
Ottawa
Pequots
Powhatans
Pueblo
Tuscarora
Wampanoags
Yamasee

Extra Challenge:

Locate the areas where each of these conflicts took place on your map of Colonial North America from Unit 1.

Close-up: The Fur Trade

The fur trade had a profound impact on the natives of northern North America. On the surface, it was a simple exchange: Trade goods for furs. This simple exchange had many complex, long-term effects. Native Americans no longer hunted fur-bearing animals for their own relatively modest needs. They trapped beaver, for example, until these creatures disappeared from entire wide areas. Using up a resource like this was completely contrary to their traditional well-balanced, respectful relationship to the environment. Accumulating private property in the form of trade goods was also a more European than Native American practice.

The fur trade also changed tribal relationships. Smaller groups allied with one another so they could control more distant areas that still had good supplies of furs. Villages relocated next to trading routes. Indian groups began fighting to control fur-trading territories. Armed with European guns, they sought to eliminate their enemies. Total war replaced limited war. Smaller tribes without European technology could no longer successfully defend themselves. The Iroquois, for example, became very powerful through their fur-trading association with the Dutch. Determined to control the fur resources of northern Canada, in the mid-1600's they attacked their old enemies the Hurons relentlessly. The Huron people, also under siege by European disease, were nearly obliterated.

Directions: From what you have read, identify the following types of effects European trade had on Native American life.

Environmental effects:

Social effects:

Economic effects:

Extra Challenge:
Identify a modern example of a sudden, new demand for a resource that has important, unexpected results.

Time Line: Indian and Colonial Wars

Directions: With classmates, construct a time line, or add to your ongoing time line, of these violent clashes among European nations and between Europeans and Native Americans. Include a brief description of each. Illustrations would make your time line more interesting.

Jamestown Massacre

Pequot War

Second Jamestown attack

New Amsterdam becomes New York

King Philip's War (Metacom's War)

Bacon's Rebellion

Pueblo uprising

King William's War

New Mexico reconquest

Queen Anne's War

Deerfield Massacre

Tuscarora War

Yamasee War

King George's War

Fort Necessity battle

Ohio Valley attacks

French and Indian War

    Fort Louisburg, Nova Scotia, falls

    Fort Duquesne becomes Fort Pitt

    Fort Niagara and Quebec fall

    Montreal falls

Treaty of Paris

Pontiac's War

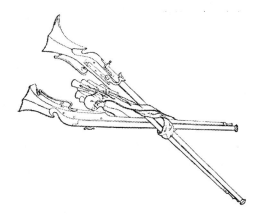

Focus on U.S. History:
The Era of Colonization and Settlement

Two Native American Views

How should Native Americans respond to the whites swarming into the lands where they lived? Opinions differed. Here are two.

Miantonomo, a Narragansett chief:

Brothers, we must be one as the English are, or we shall soon all be destroyed. You know our fathers had plenty of deer and skins, and our plains were full of deer and of turkeys, and our coves and rivers were full of fish. But, brothers, since these English have seized upon our country, they cut down the grass with scythes, and the trees with axes. Their cows and horses eat up the grass and their hogs spoil our beds of clams; and finally we shall starve to death! Therefore, stand not in your own light, I beseech you, but resolve with us to act like men. . . . We are all resolved to fall upon them, at a day appointed.

Passaconaway, a Pennacook chief:

The English came; they seized the lands; they followed upon my footpaths. I made war upon them, but they fought with fire and thunder. I, who can take the rattlesnake in my palm as I would a worm without harm—I, that have had communication with the Great Spirit, dreaming and awake—I am powerless before the palefaces. These meadows they shall turn with the plow; these forests shall fall by the axe; the palefaces shall live upon your hunting grounds and make their villages upon your fishing places. We are few and powerless before them. We must bend before the storm. Peace with the white men is the command of the Great Spirit and the wish—the last wish—of Passaconaway.

Directions: In a small group, develop answers to these questions:

- Was conflict inevitable between Europeans and Native Americans?
- How could peace be achieved?
- Was peace beneficial or harmful to Native Americans?
- What caused wars between Europeans and Native Americans?
- How did Native Americans benefit or suffer from the wars?

Then role-play a tribal council debating the advantages and disadvantages of both Passaconoway's and Miantonomo's approach to dealing with the whites. End with a vote on which course your tribal group will follow.

Focus on U.S. History:
The Era of Colonization and Settlement

The Rise of Individualism and the Seeds of Democracy

The objective of this unit is to help students understand the roots of representative government and democracy and how political rights were defined in the colonies. From the beginning, colonists in British North America were independent and self-reliant. They may have come from monarchies, but they expected to have a large voice in governing themselves. Almost all the early colonial charters provided for some participatory government, although most also set certain restrictions on political participation. Colonists from Great Britain expected to enjoy the "rights of Englishmen," certain civil rights that they were used to at home, and early colonial laws and charters incorporated some of these rights. Still, tensions remaining in some colonies between groups of settlers and their governments erupted into violent rebellion on several occasions.

Student Activities

The student background pages include an extra challenge activity. Students research the origins of the "rights of Englishmen" (optionally, as part of a small group) and present a chart of their findings.

Democracy: The Seeds Are Sown presents selections from various early charters and ordinances that set up elements of participatory government and protect certain civil rights. (You may wish to go over these selections in class to assure that all students understand them.)

The Seeds of Democracy reinforces learning though a series of comprehension questions related to the original-source material. The extra reading selection tells the intriguing story of Connecticut's charter and the Charter Oak.

Close-up: Bacon's Rebellion—and Others describes four colonial rebellions.

Colonial Rebellions provides a chart on which students identify the political, economic, social, and geographic factors that precipitated each rebellion. Students then use this information to identify a pattern in the rebellions. In the extra challenge activity, students assume the part of colonists debating the legitimacy of Bacon's Rebellion.

The Right to Vote and Hold Office sets out a number of colonial qualifications for who could vote and who could hold office in different colonies at different times.

Can You Vote? Can You Be Elected? allows students to experience the actual effects of the standards. Students assume the identity of different colonists and use the qualifications to answer "Can you vote?" and "Can you hold office?" and explain why or why not. For an extra challenge, students keep their colonial identities as they discuss why certain people should or should not be allowed to vote and hold office.

Time Line: Political Rights and Conflicts has students identify the dates of important landmarks in colonial political history. Brief descriptions and illustration enrich this activity.

The Rise of Individualism and the Seeds of Democracy

A Land of Individuals

The early colonists were, on the whole, an independent and self-reliant lot. They had to be, to leave behind life as it had been for generations and journey across a vast ocean to an unfamiliar near wilderness.

> Some were individuals willing to work hard to create a better material life for themselves and their families.
>
> Others came so they could practice their religious beliefs in the way they wanted.
>
> Transported convicts had been willing, at least once, to disobey the gentry-established law.

Once they arrived, colonists had to build their own homes, form settlements, and perhaps work a term of service to obtain economic freedom. The mother country was extremely distant, both in space and time. Plantations, towns, and even individual homesteads were often widely separated.

Under these circumstances, it's no surprise that individualism soon became a hallmark of colonial society. Colonists provided for themselves and thought for themselves. They counted on one another—not the British Army—for protection against hostile Indian attacks. European class structure was largely left behind, on the other side of the Atlantic. In colonial North America, a person—especially a white male—was usually free to make what he wanted of himself. The Jamestown colony didn't begin to thrive until settlers were granted the right to own land, so they could work for themselves instead of the colonizing company.

Self-Government Starts—Right Away

These independent-minded farmers and merchants, naturally, chose to take care of their local affairs themselves. They also expected a say in governing their colony. In Massachusetts, men drew up the Mayflower Compact aboardship in 1620, agreeing to govern themselves before they even set foot on land. In 1619, Virginia colonists elected members of a House of Burgesses to advise the governor on local affairs.

Many of the early colonial charters provided for some self-government. (Some didn't. Carolina was originally set up, on paper, as a feudal state with hereditary nobles!) How a colony's government was originally conceived made little difference. Participation soon became the norm in every colony.

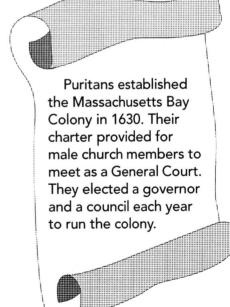

Puritans established the Massachusetts Bay Colony in 1630. Their charter provided for male church members to meet as a General Court. They elected a governor and a council each year to run the colony.

(continued)

The Rise of Individualism and
The Seeds of Democracy *(continued)*

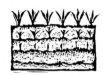

> Roger Williams left Massachusetts and founded Providence (Rhode Island) Colony in 1636. His charter, too, provided for self-government by the people of the colony.

> The 1639 Fundamental Orders of Connecticut were, in effect, a state constitution providing for self-government and the election of the governor and other public officials by the colonists.

Some colonies were settled under grants that gave vast areas of land to individual "proprietors," or owners. George Calvert, Lord Baltimore, had the right to rule as a feudal lord in Maryland. Instead, he had to allow local self-government in order to attract settlers. The same thing happened in Carolina (later North and South Carolina). New Jersey's proprietors wrote a charter that set up an elected assembly to make laws for the colony. The assembly stayed on after New Jersey became a royal colony. William Penn created an elected assembly to approve or reject proposed laws in his colony of Pennsylvania.

Out of all this, a pattern emerged. Each colony had a governor. Each colony also had a council and an assembly. The king or the governor appointed council members (except in Massachusetts), but the colonists themselves elected assembly members. Voting rights were generally restricted to white males age 21 or older. Voters commonly had to own property, but most white males did.

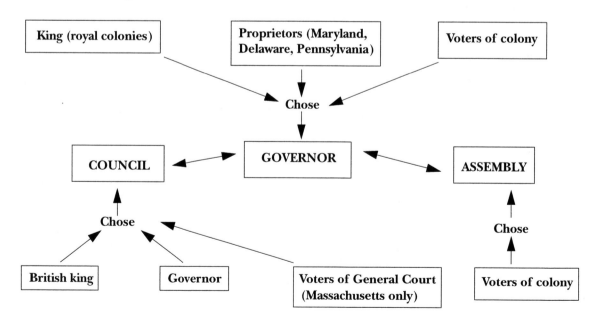

(continued)

Focus on U.S. History:
The Era of Colonization and Settlement

The Rise of Individualism and
The Seeds of Democracy *(continued)*

Elected colonial assemblies were supposed to be less powerful than the appointed governor and council. In fact, the exact opposite was true. Independent-minded colonials increasingly used their assemblies to conduct their own colonial affairs. Assemblies controlled finances in the colonies, which gave them great influence. Governors found it difficult to oppose assemblies that had the right to set a governor's salary! And back "home," in London, the British government ruled the colonies haphazardly. It had no coherent colonial policy and often ignored the rules it did set. (When England finally did try to take back control, the colonies started on the road to revolution.) England's Glorious Revolution of 1689 was an inspiration to the colonies too. Because Parliament set clear limits on the British monarch's powers, colonists felt they also could resist unreasonable royal control.

Civil Rights

In addition to these political rights, colonial charters and early laws guaranteed colonists various civil rights. Some colonies allowed religious freedom (you'll learn more about this in Unit 4). Pennsylvania and Rhode Island separated Church and State. New Jersey provided for trial by jury. Everywhere, colonists from Britain expected to enjoy the *rights of Englishmen*—liberties for all free persons that the king (or queen) couldn't take away. These included the right to a fair trial, no unjust imprisonment, free elections, and no cruel or unusual punishments.

The colonies were not democracies. But colonial life placed heavy emphasis on independence, individualism, self-government, and individual rights—all seeds of democracy.

Extra Challenge:

The "rights of Englishmen" came from English common law, the Magna Carta of 1215, and the English Bill of Rights of 1689. Research these three sources—perhaps as a member of a small group. Then make a chart showing which rights of Englishmen came from each source.

Democracy: The Seeds Are Sown

As soon as each colony was established, rules were drawn up to govern it. Many rules allowed for some type of representative government. They also protected some important civil liberties. So, early on, colonists got used to being in charge of at least some of their own affairs and having some individual rights. Here are some examples from early colonial charters, compacts, and acts.

The Mayflower Compact (1620)

(Signed aboard the *Mayflower* before going ashore at Plymouth.)
We whose names are underwritten, . . . do . . . solemnly and mutually . . . combine ourselves together into a civil body politic, for our better ordering and preservation; . . . to enact, constitute, and frame such just and equal laws . . . as shall be thought most meet and convenient for the general good of the colony, unto which we promise all due submission and obedience.

Ordinance for Virginia (1621)

The other Council . . . shall consist . . . [of the said Council of State, and] of two Burgesses out of every Town . . . to be respectively chosen by the Inhabitants. [T]his General Assembly shall have free power . . . to make, ordain, and enact such general laws and orders for the behoof [advantage] of the said colony, and the good government thereof, as shall, from time to time, appear necessary.

Massachusetts Body of Liberties (1641)

No man's life shall be taken away; no man's honor or good name shall be stained; no man's person shall be arrested, restrained, banished, dismembered, nor any way punished; no man shall be deprived of his wife or children; no man's goods or estate shall be taken away from him . . . unless it be by virtue . . . of some express law of the country.

For bodily punishments we allow among us none that are inhumane, barbarous, or cruel.

Every married woman shall be free from bodily correction or stripes [whipping] by her husband, unless it be in his own defense upon her assault.

No man shall exercise any tyranny or cruelty towards any brute creature[s] which are usually kept for man's use.

(continued)

Focus on U.S. History:
The Era of Colonization and Settlement

Democracy: The Seeds Are Sown *(continued)*

Patent of Providence Plantations (1643)

[The governor and commissioners do hereby] give, grant, and confirm to the aforesaid inhabitants . . . a free and absolute charter of incorporation.—Together with full power and authority to rule themselves . . . by such a form of civil government as by voluntary consent of all, or the greater part of them, they shall find most suitable.

Fundamental Rights of West New Jersey (1677)

(Formally titled the Concessions and Agreements—the colony's charter.)

That the common law or fundamental rights and privileges of West New Jersey are individually agreed upon by the proprietors [owners] and freeholders thereof to be the foundation of the government.

That all and every . . . persons may . . . at all times, freely and fully, have and enjoy . . . their judgments, and the exercises of their consciences, in matters of religious worship throughout all the said province.

That no proprietor, freeholder or inhabitant of the said province of West New Jersey shall be deprived or condemned of life, limb, liberty, estate, [or] property upon any account whatsoever without a due trial, and judgment passed by twelve good and lawful men of his neighborhood.

That in all matters and causes, civil and criminal, proof is to be made by the solemn and plain averment [declaration] of at least two honest and reputable persons.

That in every general free assembly, every respective member has liberty of speech. That all the justices and constables be chosen by the people.

Pennsylvania Frame of Government (1682)

That the government of this province shall consist of the governor and freemen of the said province, in form of a provincial Council and General Assembly.

That the freemen of the said province shall . . . meet and assemble in some fit place . . . and then and there shall choose out of themselves seventy-two persons . . . who shall meet . . . as the provincial Council of the said province.

. . . [T]he said freemen shall yearly choose members to serve in a General Assembly, as their representatives, not exceeding 200 persons.

That the laws . . . that are assented to by the General Assembly shall be enrolled as laws of the province.

The Seeds of Democracy

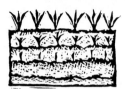

Directions: Use the information in the documents you've just read to answer these questions.

1. What model of government does the Mayflower Compact set up? _____

   _____

2. What basic principle of later U.S. government does the Mayflower Compact establish?

   _____

3. (a) Quote the lines from the Patent of Providence Plantation that express this same principle:

   _____

   (b) Quote the lines from the Fundamental Rights of West New Jersey that express this same principle:

   _____

4. (a) Who chooses members of the Virginia general assembly? _____

   _____

   (b) Who chooses members of the Pennsylvania council and general assembly?

   _____

   (c) What is the name for this type of government? _____

   _____

5. The English king expected his representatives to control the colonies. What examples do you find in these early documents that the colonists are not likely to go along with royal control?

   (a) in Massachusetts (the Mayflower Compact): _____

   _____

   (b) in Virginia: _____

   _____

   (c) in Providence: _____

   _____

(continued)

The Seeds of Democracy *(continued)*

(d) in Pennsylvania: _____

_____

Challenge Question:

Maybe the English king should have paid more attention to this issue early on! Do you think it would have been possible to keep tight royal control of the colonial governments?

---

6. (a) What basic civil rights do the Laws and Liberties of Massachusetts set in place?

_____

_____

(b) What basic civil rights do the Fundamental Rights of West New Jersey set in place?

_____

_____

The Charter Oak

Colonists took their actual physical charters seriously. Without them independent rights might not exist. In 1686 a new royal governor, Sir Edmund Andros, arrived in New England. He was supposed to establish royal rule over pesky self-governing colonies like Connecticut. How? By physically removing Connecticut's self-governing charter.

In 1687, Andros met in Hartford with Connecticut's governor and assembly to demand the charter. Discussion lasted until evening, when candles were lighted. The colonists placed their precious charter on the table in front of Andros. Suddenly, all the candles went out—darkness! When they were relighted, the charter had vanished.

According to tradition, Connecticut's constitution was hidden in the hollow of a great oak tree until the angry colonists drove Andros back to England. This story became such a legend that Connecticut was nicknamed "the Charter Oak State." Sadly, a hurricane toppled the tree in 1856. People flocked to get souvenir pieces of the famed Charter Oak.

Close-up: Bacon's Rebellion—and Others

Sometimes, the colonists' disagreements with their governments erupted into violence. Tensions boiled over in Virginia in 1676. Tobacco farming required a lot of land and labor, which meant owning slaves. Large growers soon became wealthy plantation owners. Growers of smaller farms couldn't compete. When their soil gave out, they had to move on to new lands in the colony's western frontier. The Indians who inhabited those lands naturally resisted.

The aristocratic plantation owners ran Virginia's government. They looked down on the western planters. The westerners resented this. In 1676, they asked Virginia's haughty governor, Sir William Berkeley, to authorize an action against local Indians. Berkeley refused. The planters' leader (and Berkeley's nephew), Nathaniel Bacon, led a force of about five hundred against the Indians anyway. Then Bacon marched his forces on Jamestown, got the governor's authority to fight Indians, marched back west to do that, and then returned to Jamestown and burned it. Governor Berkeley and his supporters had to flee, while Bacon's men looted and burned some of their plantations. The rebellion ended when Bacon died suddenly of a fever. Berkeley soon regained control. In revenge, he ordered 23 of Bacon's followers executed.

Leisler's Rebellion

Bacon's was not the only colonial rebellion. In 1689 Jacob Leisler, a militia leader, seized control of the New York government after King James II abandoned his throne. Leisler was a merchant who resented English rule. As New York's leader, he restored local elections and the elected assembly. He lost power in 1691 and was hanged for treason. (His sentence was later reversed.)

▲ Carolina Regulators

North Carolina, too, had a violent rebellion. Frontier settlers, the Regulators, demanded more representation in the colonial assembly. They also protested too-high taxes and corrupt local officials appointed by the royal governor. The low-country, coastal-area colonists, who ran the assembly, sent troops to fight the Regulators. They defeated the rebels in 1771 at the Battle of the Alamance.

Paxton Boys' Uprising

In 1763 settlers on Pennsylvania's western frontier rebelled. They were outnumbered in the colonial assembly. They couldn't get assembly members from eastern Pennsylvania to spend money to fight Indians in the west of the colony. A group called the Paxton Boys massacred a village of peaceful Indians. Then about six hundred western frontiersmen marched toward the capital, Philadelphia. They surrendered when a group of officials led by Benjamin Franklin agreed that they had a right to complain about their representation in the assembly. The uprising ended, but the westerners' problems weren't solved.

Colonial Rebellions

Directions: Several different factors combined to cause the colonial rebellions you've just read about. Use what you've learned to fill in this chart.

	Political Factors	Economic Factors	Social Factors	Geographic Factors
Bacon's Rebellion				
Leisler's Rebellion				
Paxton Boys' Uprising				
Carolina Regulators				

Do you see a pattern to these rebellions? Describe it: _____

_____

_____

Extra Challenge:

With classmates, role-play the part of colonists debating these questions: Was Bacon's Rebellion a justifiable attempt to change an unresponsive government's policies? Or was it a lawless attempt to overthrow a legally established government? Your role-play could be the trial of Bacon's followers, or you could be Bacon's children trying to prevent the royal government from taking all of your father's property because of his "treason."

The Right to Vote and Hold Office

Directions: Read these colonial rules about who could vote or hold office.

Pennsylvania (1682): The members of the provincial council and general assembly shall be elected by the freemen of the province. Members shall be freemen of the province.

Pennsylvania (1701): All persons who profess to believe in Jesus Christ, the Savior of the world, may serve the government in any capacity. They must promise loyalty to the King and the governor also.

Pennsylvania (1701): To vote or be elected, inhabitants of the province must 1) be freemen, 2) be 21 years or older, 3) own 50 acres of land (with 10 acres of this cleared) or otherwise have a personal estate worth at least 50 pounds [units of English money], 4) have lived in this province for at least 2 years.

Massachusetts (1691): Members of the assembly shall be freeholders elected by each town's freeholders and other inhabitants. To vote, a person must have a land estate worth at least 40 shillings per year or other personal estate worth at least 40 pounds sterling.

New Jersey (1676): The inhabitants and freeholders of this province shall meet yearly to choose freeholders to represent them in the provincial assembly.

New Jersey (1776): All inhabitants of this colony who are at least 21 years old and worth 50 pounds are entitled to vote.

New Haven (Connecticut, 1643): Only free burgesses may have any vote in any election. Only planters who are members of one of the approved churches in New England may be free burgesses.

Connecticut (1638): Public officials shall be chosen by freemen who have taken the oath of fidelity and who are inhabitants of this commonwealth.

Virginia (1646): Freemen who do not vote on election day shall be assessed a fine of 100 pounds of tobacco. Bound servants who do not exercise their right to vote are not subject to this fine.

Virginia (1670): No one but freeholders and householders shall have a voice in the election of burgesses from now on.

South Carolina (1600's): Almost any white male Protestant at least 21 years old can vote.

South Carolina (1759): Voters must be male and own 100 acres of land or have paid an annual tax of 10 shillings. Members of the lower house in the legislature must be male and own 500 acres of land and 10 slaves, or property worth 1,000 pounds.

*Focus on U.S. History:
The Era of Colonization and Settlement*

Can You Vote? Can You Be Elected?

The right to vote existed in the American colonies from their beginnings. But only certain people enjoyed this right. Not everyone could hold public office (be a member of an assembly or a constable, for example), either.

You just read some colonial rules about who could vote and hold office. "Freeholders," mentioned in the rules, were male landowners. "Householders" were male occupants of houses, where they lived alone or as a head of the household.

Directions: Suppose you are each of the following people. Use the information in the colonial rules to answer each question.

1. You are a poor laborer in Connecticut in 1645.

   Can you vote? _____

   Why or why not? _____

   _____

2. You are a black man in Pennsylvania who has been released from slavery in 1690. You do not yet own any land.

   Can you vote? _____

   Why or why not? _____

   _____

3. You are a 23-year-old woman living in New Jersey in 1777.

   Can you vote? _____

   Why or why not? _____

   _____

4. You are a 43-year-old Jewish merchant in Pennsylvania in 1705.

   Can you be elected to the provincial council?

   Why or why not? _____

   _____

5. You are a 56-year-old Roman Catholic farmer in New Haven in 1646.

   Can you vote? _____

   Why or why not? _____

6. You are an indentured servant in Jamestown, Virginia, in 1647.

   Can you vote? _____

   Why or why not? _____

   _____

(continued)

Focus on U.S. History:
The Era of Colonization and Settlement

Can You Vote? Can You Be Elected? *(continued)*

7. You own no land in New Jersey in 1680, but you do live in this colony.

   Can you vote? _____

   Why or why not? _____

   Can you hold office? _____

   Why or why not? _____

   _____

8. You are a freeman of Pennsylvania who owns 40 acres of land in 1702.

   Can you vote? _____

   Why or why not? _____

   _____

9. You are a 32-year-old Jewish woman in Pennsylvania in 1682.

   Can you be elected to the provincial council?

   Why or why not? _____

   _____

10. You are a clerk in a general store in Virginia in 1675. You live in a rented room at a boarding house. You hope to own property some day.

Can you vote? _____

Why or why not? _____

_____

11. You have purchased a 100-acre plantation in South Carolina in 1760.

   Can you vote? _____

   Why or why not? _____

   _____

   Can you be elected to the lower house of the legislature? _____

   Why or why not? _____

   _____

12. You are a farmer in South Carolina. You rent the land you farm, but you don't own any land yourself.

   Can you vote in 1740? _____

   Why or why not? _____

   Can you vote in 1760? _____

   Why or why not? _____

   _____

Challenge Questions:

(a) What trend do you notice about the colonial right to vote as the years go by?

(b) Which people seem to be excluded from the right to vote?

Extra Challenge:

With classmates, role-play a discussion among colonial people about why certain people should or should not be allowed to vote and/or hold office. Should there be a property-owning qualification to vote? Why?

Time Line: Political Rights and Conflicts

Directions: With classmates, construct a time line, or add to your ongoing time line, for these important landmarks in colonial political history. Include a brief description of each. Illustrations would make your time line more interesting.

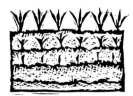

Charters, Acts, Assemblies

House of Burgesses meets for first time in Virginia

Mayflower Compact

Charter of Maryland

Fundamental Orders of Connecticut

Massachusetts Body of Liberties

Patent of Providence Plantations

Maryland Toleration Act

New Netherland self-government

Fundamental Constitutions of Carolina

Fundamental Rights of West New Jersey

Pennsylvania Frame of Government

Pennsylvania Charter of Privileges

Delaware Assembly meets

Royal charter for Georgia

Ohio Company royal charter

Rebellions

Bacon's Rebellion

Leisler's Rebellion

Paxton Boys' Uprising

Carolina Regulators' Rebellion

Events in England

Glorious Revolution

English Bill of Rights

More Seeds of Democracy

Colonists in New England decided important local matters in town meetings. Male residents of the town met, talked about, and voted on all sorts of local issues.

The male members of each individual Puritan church, or congregation, elected their church's leaders.

Religious Diversity and Freedom

The objective of this unit is for students to understand better the religious diversity in the colonies and how freedom developed to practice different kinds of religions. Some colonies were founded for religious reasons, but these did not necessarily include tolerance. Puritanism shaped New England and allowed no dissent. Other colonies, founded as a haven for people of a particular faith, offered freedom of worship for most or all others. As people of many religious faiths flocked to the colonies, religious tolerance became a practical necessity. Later, in the 1730's and 1740's, religious fervor swept the land and became the first truly "American" movement. Activities in this unit focus on better understanding of these religious aspects of colonial development.

Student Activities

Religious Immigrants introduces students to the various religious faiths immigrants from different countries brought with them to the colonies. Students are given a list of religious denominations and asked to identify their usual country of origin, their most common colonial destination, and their reason(s) for emigrating. In the mapping activity that follows, students locate and label the countries of origin and colonies of destination on their map of the Atlantic region. An extra challenge activity expands students' knowlege of colonial faiths and sects by asking for definitions (and correct spellings!) of various groups named in the Maryland Toleration Act.

A New Idea: Religious Freedom presents excerpts from colonial charters and laws related to the practice of religion. (You might wish to go over these in class to be sure all students understand them.)

In **Degrees of Religious Freedom**, students use what they have just read to identify the extent of religious freedom in different colonies and explain why each policy was established. Students will need to do some extra research to fill in some of the boxes and answer the questions.

The Puritan Way of Life quotes several Puritan leaders speaking or writing on government and social order. (Again, you may wish to go over these in class to assure all students' understanding.)

Living like a Puritan has students use what they read in these quotes to describe how Puritan ideas about authority shaped life in a Puritan community.

The Dissenters presents brief biographies of Roger Williams and Anne Hutchinson, two very important figures in the development of colonial religious freedom. Questions follow that explore reasons for religious dissent, lack of religious toleration, and separation of Church and State. In the extra challenge activity students assume the roles of colonial people to debate these issues.

Close-up: The Great Awakening tells students about this important, unifying, first "American" event.

A Famous Sermon follows up, demonstrating why Great Awakening preachers had such a powerful effect on their audiences. The extra challenge activity invites students to emulate the revivalists by finding and delivering another inspirational or emotionally moving speech on a nonreligious topic.

Religious Diversity and Freedom

Freedom to practice religion the way you wanted to did not exist in Europe during colonial times. (In fact, it never had.) Many people came to colonial North America so they could be free to worship in the way they wanted. This did *not* necessarily mean that they would be tolerant of anyone else's religious practices, though.

Several colonies were founded for religious reasons. The Pilgrims came to Plymouth, **Massachusetts**, in 1620 after they "separated" from the Church of England, which they said was corrupt. The Puritans came to Massachusetts Bay in 1630 to practice their "purified" version of the Anglican faith. They tolerated no other expression of religion. Dissenters were banished. Quakers were whipped, banished, and hanged.

When the Puritans drove Roger Williams out of their colony in 1636, he founded **Rhode Island**. It was a haven of religious toleration for all faiths. It also provided for total separation of Church and State.	**Maryland**'s charter holders, George and Cecilius Calvert, were Roman Catholic. They made their colony open to all Christians.	William Penn was a Quaker. Members of his faith were persecuted in England as well as New England. He established **Pennsylvania** colony with a policy of freedom of worship.

Other Quakers set up **New Jersey**, with a policy like the one in Pennsylvania.

Other colonies were set up primarily for profit. (Penn and the Calverts expected to profit from their colonies, too.) Even these offered freedom of worship to some degree. **Georgia** guaranteed free religious practice to all. The **Carolinas** charter named the Church of England as the official church but allowed practice of all other religions as well. Upper-class Virginians tended to be Anglican. But **Virginia** and other colonies needed to attract settlers. The best policy was to allow free practice of religion, so no valuable settlers would stay away.

The earliest colonists were mostly from England. So they were Anglicans or "reformed Anglicans"—Pilgrims and Puritans. There were also British Roman Catholics and Quakers, who faced many religious difficulties at home. Later, other religious groups poured into the colonies. So many religious groups living together made religious toleration a practical necessity.

(continued)

Focus on U.S. History:
The Era of Colonization and Settlement

Religious Diversity and Freedom *(continued)*

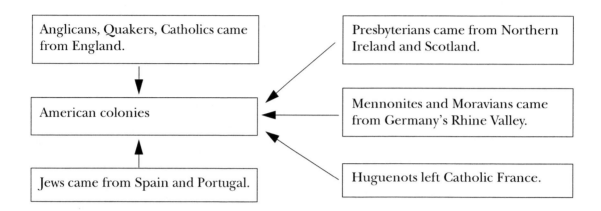

Anglicans, Quakers, Catholics came from England.		Presbyterians came from Northern Ireland and Scotland.
American colonies		Mennonites and Moravians came from Germany's Rhine Valley.
Jews came from Spain and Portugal.		Huguenots left Catholic France.

The Puritans *really* didn't like Quakers. (Quakers didn't accept the authority of the church. They wouldn't swear oaths of loyalty to the king either.) They strip-searched, then banished two Quaker women, Ann Austin and Mary Fisher, who'd come to Boston from Barbados in 1656. They whipped an old man named William Brand 117 lashes with a tarred rope until he passed out. In 1659 a Quaker couple couldn't pay fines they owed, so a Massachusetts court ordered their children to be sold into bondage and shipped to the West Indies! This Quaker story had a happy ending. No New England shipmaster would carry out the order, and the youngsters were released.

Religious Immigrants

The desire to practice their religion as they wished inspired many people to emigrate to North America.

Directions: For each religious group listed, identify the following:

• the European country they usually came from;

• the colony or colonies where they most often settled;

• reason(s) why they would have wanted to leave Europe.

Then, on the map of the Atlantic region, locate and label the countries of origin and colonies of destination you have identified.

1. **Pilgrims**   Usual country of origin: _____

   Common colony/colonies settled in: _____

   Why they emigrated: _____

2. **Anglicans**   Usual country of origin: _____

   Common colony/colonies settled in: _____

   Why they emigrated: _____

3. **Puritans**   Usual country of origin: _____

   Common colony/colonies settled in: _____

   Why they emigrated: _____

4. **Huguenots**   Usual country of origin: _____

   Common colony/colonies settled in: _____

   Why they emigrated: _____

5. **Dutch Reformed Church members**   Usual country of origin: _____

   Common colony/colonies settled in: _____

   Why they emigrated: _____

6. **Roman Catholics**   Usual country of origin: _____

   Common colony/colonies settled in: _____

   Why they emigrated: _____

(continued)

Religious Immigrants *(continued)*

7. **Quakers**   Usual country of origin: _____

   Common colony/colonies settled in:_____

   Why they emigrated: _____

8. **Presbyterians**   Usual country of origin: _____

   Common colony/colonies settled in: _____

   Why they emigrated: _____

9. **Mennonites and Moravians**   Usual country of origin: _____

   Common colony/colonies settled in: _____

   Why they emigrated: _____

10. **Jews**   Usual country of origin: _____

    Common colony/colonies settled in: _____

    Why they emigrated: _____

11. **Lutherans**   Usual country of origin: _____

    Common colony/colonies settled in: _____

    Why they emigrated: _____

Questions:

12. What two main types of religious faiths were not tolerated in France, Portugal, and Spain?

    _____

13. What belief and standard of conduct did Mennonites, Moravians, and Quakers share?

    _____

Extra Challenge: The Maryland Toleration Act provided for punishment of anyone who called anyone else within the province any of these names, in "a reproachful manner relating to religion." Tell what each of these is. (For double credit, correct the spelling!)

> ". . . an heretick, Scismatick, Idolator, puritan, Independant, Prespiterian popish prest, Jesuite, Jesuited papist, Lutheran, Calvenist, Anabaptist, Brownist, Antinomian, Barrowist, Roundhead, Seperatist . . ."

Focus on U.S. History:
The Era of Colonization and Settlement

A New Idea: Religious Freedom

Most colonial charters and early laws had something to say about the practice of religion. Here are some examples. After studying them, add the dates to the time line you created in Unit 3.

Maryland Toleration Act ("An Act Concerning Religion," 1649)

No person or persons whatsoever within this province, professing to believe in Jesus Christ, shall from henceforth be anyway troubled, [or] molested . . . for or in respect of his or her religion, nor in the free exercise thereof . . . nor any way compelled to the belief or exercise of any other religion against his or her consent.

Charter of Rhode Island and Providence Plantations (1663)

Our royal will and pleasure is, that no person within the said colony, at any time hereafter, shall be any wise molested, punished, disquieted, or called in question for any differences in opinion in matters of religion.

New Jersey Concessions (1664–65)

That all and every . . . person and persons may . . . at all times, freely and fully have and enjoy his and their judgments and consciences in matters of religion throughout the said province, they behaving themselves peaceably and quietly.

Second Charter of Massachusetts (1691)

We do . . . ordain that forever hereafter there shall be a liberty of conscience allowed in the worship of God to all Christians (except papists) inhabiting . . . within our said province.

(continued)

*Focus on U.S. History:
The Era of Colonization and Settlement*

A New Idea: Religious Freedom *(continued)*

New Haven Government (1643)

None shall be admitted to be free burgesses in any of the plantations within this jurisdiction for the future, but such planters as are members of some or other of the approved churches in New England.

Charter of Georgia (1732)

We do . . . ordain, that forever hereafter, there shall be a liberty of conscience allowed in the worship of God, to all persons inhabiting . . . our said province, and that all such persons, except papists, shall have a free exercise of religion.

Fundamental Constitutions of Carolina (1669–70)

Any seven or more persons, agreeing in any religion, shall constitute a church or profession. . . . No person of any other church or profession shall disturb or molest any religious assembly. . . . No person whatsoever shall disturb, molest, or persecute another for his speculative opinions in religion, or his way of worship.

Pennsylvania Charter of Privileges (1701)

I do hereby grant and declare, that no person or persons inhabiting in this province or territories, who shall confess and acknowledge one almighty God, the Creator, . . . shall be in any case molested or prejudiced . . . because of his or their conscientious persuasion or practice, nor be compelled to frequent or maintain any religious worship, place or ministry contrary to his or their mind.

New Amsterdam Regulations (1624)

[The colonists] shall practice no other form of divine worship within their territory than that of the Reformed religion as presently practiced here in this country, . . . without, however, persecuting anyone because of his faith, but leaving to everyone the freedom of his conscience.

(continued)

A New Idea: Religious Freedom *(continued)*

Why Allow Freedom of Worship?

Why did the colonies opt for a great deal of toleration, allowing people to practice a variety of religious faiths? The Fundamental Constitutions of Carolina spell out the answer, which is quite practical. (Note that the founders of Carolina embraced the Church of England as the "only true and orthodox" religious practice. These reasons reflect that point of view.)

[Because] the natives of that place [Carolina] are utterly strangers to Christianity, whose idolatry, ignorance, or mistake, gives us no right to expel, or use them ill;

[Because] those who remove from other parts to plant there, will unavoidably be of different opinions concerning matters of religion, the liberty whereof they will expect to have allowed them, and it will not be reasonable for us on this account to keep them out;

[So that] civil peace may be maintained amidst the diversity of opinions, and our agreement and compact with all men may be duly and faithfully observed; the violation whereof, upon what pretense whatsoever, cannot be without great offense to Almighty God, and great scandal to true religion, which we profess;

[And also because] Jews, heathens, and other dissenters from the purity of the Christian religion may not be scared and kept at a distance from it, but by having an opportunity of acquainting themselves with the truth and reasonableness of its doctrines, and the peaceableness and inoffensiveness of its professors, may . . . be won over to embrace and . . . receive the truth.

Focus on U.S. History:
The Era of Colonization and Settlement

Degrees of Religious Freedom

Directions: From what you have read, identify the degree of religious freedom in different colonies by filling in the boxes below. (You may have to do a bit of extra research for this.)

Colony	Which Religions Were Allowed?	Why Was This Policy Established?
Massachusetts		
Rhode Island		
New Netherland		
Pennsylvania		
New Jersey		
Maryland		
Virginia		
Carolinas		
New Haven		
Georgia		

Questions:

1. Was Massachusetts really tolerant of all religious faiths? _____

_____

2. Were non-Christians or atheists driven out of colonies that didn't grant full freedom of religious expression? _____

_____

Focus on U.S. History:
The Era of Colonization and Settlement

The Puritan Way of Life

The Puritans intended to create a holy community, ruled by God's laws. Here are some leading Puritans' ideas about government and social order.

The authority possessed by kings and other governors over all things upon earth is not a consequence of the perverseness of men, but of the providence and holy ordinance of God; who hath been pleased to regulate human affairs in this manner. . . . The obedience which is rendered to princes and magistrates is rendered to God, from whom they have received their authority. . . . [So] it is impossible to resist the magistrate without, at the same time, resisting God himself.

—John Calvin (1559)

For husbands owe mutual duties to their wives, and parents to their children. Now, if husbands and parents violate their obligations, if parents conduct themselves with discouraging severity and fastidious moroseness towards their children, whom they are forbidden to provoke to wrath; if husbands despise and vex their wives, whom they are commanded to love and to spare as the weaker vessels; does it follow that children should be less obedient to their parents; or wives to their husbands? They are still subject, even to those who are wicked and unkind.

—John Calvin (1559)

It is better that the commonwealth be fashioned to the setting forth of God's house, which is his church, than to accommodate the church frame to the civil state. Democracy, I do not conceive that ever God did ordain as a fit government either for church or commonwealth. If the people be governors, who shall be governed? . . . [I see] theocracy . . . as the best form of government in the commonwealth, as well as in the church.

—Reverend John Cotton (1636)

If you stand for your natural and corrupt liberties, and will do what is good in your own eyes, you will not endure the least weight of authority, but will murmur, and oppose, and be always striving to shake off that yoke. But if you will be satisfied to enjoy such civil and lawful liberties, such as Christ allows you, then will you quietly and cheerfully submit unto that authority which is set over you, in all the administrations of it, for your good.

—John Winthrop, Governor of Massachusetts (1645)

Theocratic, or to make the Lord God our Governor, is the best form of government in a Christian commonwealth, and which men that are free to choose . . . ought to establish. . . . [Theocracy is] that form of government where: (1) The people that have the power of choosing their governors are in covenant with God. (2) Wherein the men chosen by them are godly men, and fitted with a spirit of government. (3) In which the laws they rule by are the laws of God. (4) Wherein laws are executed, inheritances allotted, and civil differences are composed, according to God's appointment. (5) In which men of God are consulted with in all hard cases, and in matters of religion.

—Reverend John Davenport (1638)

51

*Focus on U.S. History:
The Era of Colonization and Settlement*

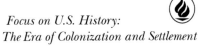

Living like a Puritan

Directions: From what you have read about Puritans' ideas, describe what life in a Puritan community might be like in the following areas.

1. Individual expression, opinion, action

2. Role of magistrates (local governing officials)

3. Role of ministers, religious leaders

4. Role of the people in government

5. Authority within the family

More on Puritan Husbands and Wives: Here's another expression of the relationship between husbands and wives, written by Puritan leader John Winthrop in 1654:

The woman's own choice makes [such] a man her husband; yet being so chosen, he is her lord, and she is to be subject to him, yet in a way of liberty, not of bondage; and a true wife accounts her subjection her honor and freedom, and would not think her condition safe and free, but in her subjection to her husband's authority. Such is the liberty of the church under the authority of Christ, her king and husband; his yoke is so easy and sweet to her as a bride's ornaments; and if through forwardness or wantonness, etc., she shake it off, at any time, she is at no rest in her spirit, until she take it up again; and whether her lord smiles upon her, and embraces her in his arms, or whether he frowns, or rebukes, or smites her, she apprehends the sweetness of his love in all, and is refreshed, supported, and instructed by every such dispensation of his authority over her.

The Dissenters

Not all Puritans toed the rigid line of belief drawn by the Puritan leaders. Members of the church who wouldn't conform were booted out of the colony. Here are the stories of two of these dissenters.

Roger Williams

Roger Williams came to Massachusetts in 1631. He'd been ordained a minister in the Church of England in London. When he became a Puritan, he brought his family to Boston. He was elected minister of the church at Salem in 1635, but his strange ideas began to bother his fellow Puritans. He said that civil government—the Puritans' magistrates—had no right to enforce any religious laws. He insisted that no one, not even the king of England, had the right to take any colonial land without purchasing it from the Native Americans. He demanded that the Massachusetts church separate from the Church of England, which was not "pure."

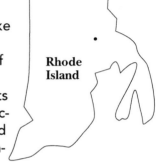

Rhode Island

Williams refused to give up any of his "errors." So the Massachusetts General Court ordered him expelled from the colony to keep his "infection" from spreading. An arrest warrant called for Williams to be forced to board a ship and return to London. Instead, he fled to the Narragansett Bay area in January 1636. He purchased land there from local Indians who helped him survive the winter. He founded the settlement of Providence, which became the colony of Rhode Island when Williams got a charter for it, in 1644.
In Rhode Island, Williams was able to set up the type of society he had dreamed of. His colony had representative government—all landowners could vote and choose their own type of government. The people of Rhode Island had complete religious freedom. Church and State were completely separate. Rhode Island became a haven for people who were seldom welcome anywhere else in the colonies, like Quakers and Jews. Williams's fair and just relations with the native Indians ensured peaceful coexistence for all within the colony.

Extra Challenge:

Role-play the trial of Roger Williams or Anne Hutchinson. The two dissenters (and perhaps their followers) should justify their actions. The members of the Massachusetts General Court should state their objections and why each dissenter must be banished from the colony. Be emphatic! These were court cases that aroused a lot of controversy and emotion when they were going on.

(continued)

The Dissenters *(continued)*

Anne Hutchinson

Anne Hutchinson also caused headaches for the Puritan leaders. She too was born in England, where she married her husband William in 1612. They came to Massachusetts in 1634 with their brood of children, which eventually totaled 15. Hutchinson soon began developing ideas that were at odds with the established Puritan powers. She believed in saving grace and direct spiritual communication between individuals and God. Such saved people didn't have to observe religious laws, Hutchinson said. She also interpreted the Bible for herself and criticized the Boston ministers' sermons.

Trial of Anne Hutchinson

Hutchinson, a brilliant and well-spoken woman, developed quite a following. The Puritan leaders became alarmed. She was charged with the heresy of **antinomianism** (which means "against the law"), or saying that believers are not bound by moral law. As with Williams, the court banished Hutchinson from the colony in 1638. With her husband, many children, and some followers, she settled at Pocasset, in what was then Rhode Island. Even there, Hutchinson clashed with other settlers. After her husband died, in 1642, she moved with six of her children to Pelham Bay, in New Netherland. Indians killed all but the youngest Hutchinson girl there in 1643.

Questions:

1. How did Williams and Hutchinson violate the rules of their Puritan communities?

   _____

   _____

2. Why did Puritan leaders think that Williams and Hutchinson had to be banished?

   _____

   _____

3. What important principle of our government did Roger Williams first put into practice and law?

   _____

Close-up: The Great Awakening

Religion played a very important part in bringing early settlers to the colonies and in many early colonial societies. But by the beginning of the 1700's, religion was no longer such a big factor in colonial life. The booming colonial economy made settlers focus on the rewards of this life instead of the hereafter. As trade and towns grew, so did nonreligious outside influences. Young people were drifting away from the piety of their parents and grandparents.

Religious fervor began to revive in the 1720's. The revival movement, known as the Great Awakening, swept the colonies. It peaked in the 1740's. Dramatic traveling preachers worked their listeners up to states of high emotion. Theodorus Frelinghuysen caused Dutch Reformed congregations all through New Jersey to tremble before visions of hellfire and damnation. Gilbert Tennent, a Scotch-Irish Presbyterian, denounced sin and sinners with great zeal in Pennsylvania and New Jersey. George Whitefield, an English Anglican minister, was a dramatic, electrifying orator. He began touring the colonies, filling churches everywhere, in 1738. A wave of emotional religious response swept through the land with him. Jonathan Edwards reawakened New England's religious fervor. His famous sermon "Sinners in the Hands of an Angry God" treated his listeners to a vivid description of the terrors of hell—which many of them would surely taste, he added.

Intense enthusiasms, no matter how exciting they are, fade after a time. The Great Awakening and revivalist preaching began to dwindle after 1750. But the movement had important effects. It was the first really "American" event. All the colonies were united in a common enthusiasm. Also, revivalist preachers drew followers away from more conservative clergy. Converts learned to resist outside authority and rely on their own experience. Radical church groups split off from established ones. This rebellious spirit would stay alive as the American Revolution approached.

Charles Chauncey, pastor of Boston's First Church, did *not* approve of revivalist preaching. He described it in 1743:

"The next thing I shall take notice of, as what I can't but think of dangerous tendency, is that terror so many have been the subjects of; expressing itself in strange effects upon the body, such as swooning away and falling to the ground, where persons have lain, for a time, speechless and motionless; bitter shriekings, screamings, convulsion-like tremblings, agitations, strugglings, and tumblings, which, in some instances have been attended with indecencies I shan't mention."

Charles Chauncey tells how people felt in the midst of their frenzy:

"Some say, they had presented to their View, at the time, a sight of their sins, in all their number; others, that they saw hell, as it were, naked before them, and destruction without a covering; and that it seemed to them as though they were just falling into it. Others, that they imagined the devils were about them, and ready to lay hold on them, and draw them away to hell. The general account is, that they were filled with great anxiety and distress, having upon their minds an overpowering sense of sin, and fear of divine wrath."

*Focus on U.S. History:
The Era of Colonization and Settlement*

A Famous Sermon

Jonathan Edwards was a brilliant, intellectual Puritan minister. He was also the most famous revivalist preacher of the Great Awakening. He wanted to shock members of his congregation into being "born again" and having a revelation of "saving grace." Here's a sample of his approach. This is an excerpt from Edwards's most famous sermon, "Sinners in the Hands of an Angry God." As he delivered these terrifying words in his Enfield, Connecticut, church in 1741, listeners in the congregation began moaning and crying out. Can you see why people who heard all of this sermon might react in the way Charles Chauncey describes?

There is nothing that keeps wicked men at any one moment out of hell but the mere pleasure of God. . . . [E]very unconverted man properly belongs to hell; that is his place. . . .

The wrath of God burns against [all unconverted people]; their damnation does not slumber; the pit is prepared; the fire is made ready; the furnace is now hot; ready to receive them; the flames do now rage and glow. The glittering sword is whet and held over them, and the pit hath opened her mouth under them. The devil stands ready to fall upon them and seize them as his own, at what moment God shall permit him. . . . The devils watch them; they are ever by them, at their right hand; they stand waiting for them like greedy hungry lions that see their prey and expect to have it, but are for the present kept back. . . .

The God that holds you over the pit of hell, much as one holds a spider or some loathsome insect over the fire, abhors you, and is dreadfully provoked. His wrath toward you burns like fire; he looks upon you as worthy of nothing else but to be cast into the fire. . . .

O sinner! consider the fearful danger you are in: it is a great furnace of wrath, a wide and bottomless pit, full of the fire of wrath, that you are held over in the hand of that God, whose wrath is provoked and incensed as much against you as many of the damned in hell. You hang by a slender thread, with the flames of divine wrath flashing about it, and ready every moment to singe it and burn it asunder. . . .

How dreadful is the state of those that are daily and hourly in danger of this great wrath and infinite misery! But this is the dismal case of every soul in this congregation that has not been born again, however moral and strict, sober and religious they may otherwise be. . . . The wrath of Almighty God is now undoubtedly hanging over a great part of this congregation. . . . How can you rest one moment in such a condition?

Extra Challenge:

Find some other, nonreligious speeches made by a figure in history, or in present times, that were intended to inspire the listeners or move them emotionally. Then deliver the speech, or parts of it, to classmates. Be emotional! Act the part! Try to get an emotional reaction from your listeners.

Social and Cultural Life

This unit is designed to give students a better understanding of the social and cultural life of British North America. Family and community life varied from region to region and situation to situation. For example, life on a New England or frontier subsistence farm was quite different from life on a large middle-colony farm or on a southern plantation. Rules of behavior were particularly strict in New England. Still, all colonists amused themselves in various ways, and educated men enjoyed a lively exchange of ideas. Public education came early to the colonies, particularly the closely knit towns of New England. Activities in this unit explore the social and cultural life of the colonies and how it indicated the emergence of a new American character.

Student Activities

Men's Work, Women's Work, Children's Work presents a sample of the many never-ending chores a colonial subsistence-farming family had to perform and reveals gender specificity of different tasks. You should guide students to note that division of work by gender was practical, given the immense amount of manual labor on the farm, and that all family members were partners making valuable contributions to the family enterprise.

Life in New England will amuse most students. Related activities are suggested in the Answer Key, Additional Activities, Assessment section at the back of this book.

Colonial Houses uses architecture to underscore regional differences.

Crime and Punishment helps students understand colonial mores by matching punishments with crimes. The punishments seem extreme by modern standards, but they weren't unduly harsh for those times. Also, many colonial leaders (especially Puritans) believed that establishing a new community in the wilderness required behavior to be strictly regulated if society was to survive.

Time Line: Social and Cultural Life lists important educational, literary, religious-cultural, and scientific-intellectual landmarks in colonial history. Students are required to find dates for each.

Benjamin Franklin: An American Original introduces students to Franklin's down-to-earth philosophy. They identify which character traits "Poor Richard" admired and scorned and from them extrapolate a definition of the emerging American character reflected in Franklin's work, noting how it differed from the popular conception of "typically" European. For an extra challenge students can write their own Franklinesque aphorisms.

How They Lived presents contemporary descriptions of life in different colonial areas. (You may wish to go over these in class to assure that all students understand them.) A group activity based on the reading follows. It asks students to develop a rounded report on social and cultural life in a particular colonial region or town and can serve as a unit assessment.

Social and Cultural Life

New England

Family and community life differed from region to region in colonial North America. Most people in New England were farmers. They clustered their farms together into little settlements because of the danger of Indian attack. These farm families were self-sufficient—they produced almost everything they needed, in spite of New England's thin, rocky soil. Everyday life was a nearly endless round of chores, for all family members. Other New Englanders lived in larger towns, like Boston, a lively seaport. Life there revolved around trade, shipping, and fishing.

Puritan life was very strict. So it's somewhat surprising that the practice of **bundling** was accepted. Here's how it worked: A courting boy and girl in New England wanted to be alone. But the family was all gathered around the fireplace. The rest of the house was frigid. What to do? They'd retire to an out-of-the-way bed, fully clothed, and whisper sweet nothings to each other there—separated by a "bundling board" that extended down the center of the bed.

The Puritan way of life dominated New England during the early colonial days. Religion affected every part of life. Laws and rules for behavior were based on religion. Everyone was expected to live a proper moral life at all times. Children were expected to obey their parents completely. Wives had to obey their husbands. But as towns and trade grew, life got easier. It was no longer such a struggle for survival. The children and grandchildren of the Puritans relaxed a bit. They focused more on their own lives than on the word of God. So the Puritan hold on New England society gradually declined. Still, Puritan emphasis on thrift, hard work, and living life as you see fit remains a hallmark of the Yankee character.

Middle Colonies

The middle colonies were a mix of people from many different ethnic and religious origins. All lived comfortably together because the middle colonies were quite prosperous. Pennsylvania, New Jersey, and Delaware had been founded on principles of toleration. Community and family life there varied considerably. Farm families lived on large scattered holdings. Going beyond self-sufficiency, these farmers made life more comfortable by raising cash crops on their fertile soil for sale in nearby markets. Other families lived in towns, both large and small. Heads of household worked in the many manufacturing, iron mining, shipbuilding, and craft jobs spread around the middle colonies. German Mennonites and Moravians lived communally. Independent rebellious newcomers roughed it in the frontier backcountry.

Southern Colonies

The southern colonies also had their backcountry. Families and individuals eked out a hard existence there as farmers, hunters, and trappers. The tidewater region of the South was a plantation society. A large plantation was like a little town. The planter and his family lived in a big house, perhaps a mansion. Many small buildings near the great house were devoted to special tasks—cooking, schooling, making bricks, baking, laundry, and smoking meats. Slaves had their own quarters and their own quite distinct society. *(continued)*

Learning your colonial ABC's could be a bit grim. Here are a few verses from the widely used *New England Primer.*
Job feels the rod,
Yet blesses God.

The idle **F**ool
Is whipped at school.

The **C**at doth play And after slay.

Learning the ABC's

Regional differences affected how different colonies handled education for children. A central part of Puritan religious practice was reading the Bible. So children had to learn to read. The Massachusetts Bay Colony School Law of 1642 required parents to teach their children "so much learning as may enable them perfectly to read the English tongue." Parents who weren't up to this sent their children to a "dame school," taught by a local woman in her home. Massachusetts also made it law that every town with 50 families or more had to set up a public school. Connecticut soon followed suit. These grammar schools were for boys only, to prepare them for college. Girls stayed home and learned domestic skills.

In the South, plantations and farms were widely scattered. A central public school wasn't possible, so southern parents taught their own children how to read and write (if the parents knew how themselves). Well-off planters would hire a tutor to live on the plantation and teach their children, and maybe the children of neighbors and relatives. Black slaves got no formal education at all.

If you were a Puritan lad or lass, you might look forward to a bit of dancing. Oops! Here's what Increase Mather, a leading Puritan minister, had to say about that:
"But our question is concerning . . . mixed or promiscuous dancing, viz., men and women . . . together. Now this we affirm to be utterly unlawful and that it cannot be tolerated in such a place as New England without great sin. . . . The unchaste touches and gesticulations used by dancers have a palpable tendency to that which is evil. . . . [S]uch a practice is a scandalous immorality."

Amusements

Colonial life wasn't all work. Farm families turned tasks like husking corn into community parties. Children played games of all kinds—when they weren't doing their many chores. In their homes, many families enjoyed music, dancing, and simple skits and plays (except in Puritan Massachusetts, which outlawed such frivolous pursuits). Wealthy families put on fancy-dress balls or elaborate dinners for hordes of guests. Many men who had the benefit of an education kept a lifelong interest in learning. They studied, discussed, and wrote about science, philosophy, natural science, literature, political theory, and other topics. This exchange helped circulate independent, even radical, ideas about how society, government, and religion ought to be structured.

Colonial Women: During colonial times, husbands ruled their families. When a woman married, both she and her property came under her husband's control. However, the reality of colonial life made wives relatively equal partners with their husbands. The jobs a woman did on a colonial farm were vital and highly valued, as were a man's. A southern planter was fully engaged in managing his vast farm and his many workers. A planter's wife had an equally large job managing the sprawling household and many visitors. Widows and wives whose husbands were ill often ran their husbands' businesses.

Men's Work, Women's Work, Children's Work

Colonial families living in farming towns or on their own in isolated frontier settlements had a lot of work to do! They produced almost everything they needed right there, by themselves. Labor was mostly divided: Men did certain jobs; women did others. This was an efficient way to get everything done. Children helped.

Directions: Try to identify who did each of the tasks listed below. Write men, women, or children in the space provided.

Clearing land	Planting crops
Making butter	Making cheese
Making soap	Plowing fields
Chopping up firewood	Making beer and cider
Spinning yarn	Creating clothing
Butchering cattle	Harvesting crops
Butchering chickens	Hunting for wild game
Building and mending fences	Milking cows
Washing clothes	Hauling water
Cooking meals	Weaving wool into cloth
Making iron tools	Shearing sheep
Hoeing, weeding, tending the kitchen garden	Dying fabric

Life in New England

Here's a humorous but realistic description of life in early New England. It's a colonial ballad that dates back to around 1630.

Forefathers' Song

New England's annoyances you that would
    know them,
Pray ponder these verses which briefly doth
    show them.
The place where we live is a wilderness wood,
Where grass is much wanting that's fruitful
    and good:
Our mountains and hills and our valleys below,
Being commonly covered with ice and with
    snow;
And when the north-west wind with violence
    blows,
Then every man pulls his cap over his nose:
But if any's so hardy and will it withstand,
He forfeits a finger, a foot or a hand.

But when the Spring opens we then take
    the hoe,
And make the ground ready to plant and
    to sow;
Our corn being planted and seed being sown,
The worms destroy much before it is grown;
And when it is growing, some spoil there
    is made
By birds and by squirrels that pluck up
    the blade;
And when it is come to full corn in the ear,
It is often destroyed by raccoon and by deer.

And now our garments begin to grow thin,
And wool is much wanted to card and to spin;
If we can get a garment to cover without,
Our other in-garments are clout [patch]
    upon clout:
Our clothes we brought with us are apt to
    be torn,

They need to be clouted soon after they're
    worn,
But clouting our garments they hinder us
    nothing,
Clouts double are warmer than single whole
    clothing.

If fresh meat be wanting to fill up our dish,
We have carrots and turnips as much as
    we wish:
And if there's a mind for a delicate dish
We repair to the clam-banks, and there we
    catch fish.
Instead of pottage and puddings and custards
    and pies,
Our pumpkins and parsnips are common
    supplies;
We have pumpkins at morning and pumpkins
    at noon,
If it was not for pumpkins we should be
    undone!
If barley be wanting to make into malt,
We must be contented, and think it no fault;
For we can make liquor to sweeten our lips,
Of pumpkins and parsnips and walnut-tree
    chips.

Focus on U.S. History:
The Era of Colonization and Settlement

Colonial Houses

Directions: The typical colonial house varied from region to region. See if you can match each colonial home with its description, written by an actual colonial traveler. Draw a line from each description to the home it matches. Also, tell in which colonial region you'd be likely to find each home.

A large, elegant house, built with brick; 76 feet long and 44 feet wide, 2 stories high; it has 5 stacks of chimneys, though 2 of these serve only for ornament. There is a beautiful projection on the south side, 18 feet long and 8 feet deep, supported by 3 tall pillars.

Region: _____

The houses are made of thin, small cedar shingles, nailed against wooden frames, and then filled in with brick and other stuff. Or they are covered with wooden clapboards. They are for the most part two stories high, mostly sashed. Some are of the saltbox style, two stories high in the front, with a steeply pitched roof in the rear.

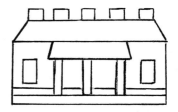

Region: _____

Most of the houses in this part of the country are loghouses, the logs being notched at the ends and fitted together. Their doors turn upon wooden hinges and have wooden locks to secure them, so that the building is finished without nails or other ironwork.

Region: _____

This little hut was one of the wretchedest I ever saw as a habitation for human creatures. It was supported with shores enclosed with clapboards, laid on lengthways, and so much asunder, that the light came through everywhere. The door was tied on with a cord in place of hinges. The floor was the bare earth.

Region: _____

*Focus on U.S. History:
The Era of Colonization and Settlement*

Crime and Punishment

Directions: Colonial punishments for wrongdoing seem harsh by today's standards. See if you can match each colonial crime below with its punishment. Write the letter of the punishment next to the number of the crime.

Crime	Punishment
1. ___ live as an idler (don't work)	(a) public whipping
2. ___ have a child out of wedlock (the mother)	(b) nostrils are slit and burned; pay a fine
3. ___ have a child out of wedlock (the father)	(c) pay a 20-shilling fine
4. ___ be drunk	(d) be warned three times; pay a 5-shilling fine the fourth time
5. ___ slander someone (make "base and detracting" remarks)	(e) hand is branded with a T
6. ___ be a scold or a gossip	(f) be appointed [assigned to] a master to serve for wages
7. ___ pass counterfeit money	(g) arms are broken, tongue is bored through with an awl; banishment from colony
8. ___ rape a woman	(h) be locked in the stocks for 12 hours on the third offense
9. ___ commit adultery	(i) be dunked underwater in the dunking stool
10. ___ be a traitor against the government	(j) death or public humiliation
11. ___ swearing (a freeman)	(k) pay fines and child support
12. ___ swearing (a servant)	(l) be warned three times; be whipped the fourth time
13. ___ petty larceny (minor theft)	(m) 30 lashes on the naked back
14. ___ grand larceny (major theft)	(n) be hanged, then drawn and quartered
15. ___ wearing silk, lace, or gold/silver buttons if you're worth less than £200	(o) 3-shilling fine each time
16. ___ swearing against the church	(p) one ear cut off, 20 stripes at the public whipping-post, and 1 hour in the pillory
17. ___ failing to attend Sabbath services both morning and afternoon	(q) ears cut off, whipping, banishment

Name _____

Date _____

Time Line: Social and Cultural Life

Directions: Add these important social and cultural landmarks in colonial times to the time line you have constructed in other units.

Education Laws
Massachusetts Bay Colony school law
Plymouth Colony school law (a school for every town with at least 50 families)
Connecticut school law (a school for every town with at least 50 families)

Colleges are founded
Harvard College
the College of William and Mary
the Collegiate School in New Haven (becomes Yale)
the College of New Jersey (becomes Princeton)
King's College (becomes Columbia)
the College of Philadelphia (becomes the University of Pennsylvania)
Rhode Island College (becomes Brown University)
Queen's College (becomes Rutgers)
Dartmouth College

Publications
the *New England Primer*
John Smith's *A True Relation . . . of Virginia*
Poor Richard's Almanack
John Eliot's Bible in the Algonquian language

Religious and Cultural Events
the Great Awakening
Jonathan Edwards's sermon "Sinners in the Hands of an Angry God"

Science and Intellectual Life
Franklin invents the Franklin stove
Franklin conducts kite experiment with lightning and electricity
Rittenhouse builds an orrery
North American colonies' first modern hospital, in Philadelphia

Challenge Question: What is an orrery?

Focus on U.S. History:
The Era of Colonization and Settlement

Benjamin Franklin: An American Original

Benjamin Franklin was an amazing man. He invented many useful things, like bifocal glasses and the lightning rod. He was a scientist, an ambassador, a politician, a thinker, a newspaper publisher, and a writer. He began his career by running away from his Boston apprenticeship with his older half-brother. Settled in Philadelphia, Franklin became very wealthy when he began publishing his highly popular *Poor Richard's Almanack,* in 1732. The almanac gave a lot of weather information and predictions. It also contained many sayings and bits of advice written by Franklin that give a good picture of the new, independent, hardworking colonial person.

Directions: In your own words, explain what character traits each of these Poor Richard sayings praises or criticizes.

1. Speak little, do much. _____
   _____
   _____

2. When the wine enters, out goes the truth.
   _____
   _____
   _____

3. A plowman on his legs is higher than a gentleman on his knees. _____
   _____
   _____

4. God heals, and the doctor takes the fees.
   _____
   _____
   _____

5. Beware of little expenses; a small leak will sink a great ship. _____
   _____
   _____

6. He that hath a trade, hath an estate. ____
   _____

7. Neglect mending a small fault, and it will soon be a great one. _____
   _____
   _____

8. In rivers and bad governments, the lightest things swim at top. _____
   _____
   _____

9. Dally not with other folk's women or money.
   _____
   _____

10. Wealth and content are not always bedfellows.
    _____
    _____

11. Fish and visitors stink in three days. _____
    _____
    _____

12. Having been poor is no shame, but being ashamed of it is. _____
    _____
    _____

(continued)

Benjamin Franklin: An American Original *(continued)*

13. Don't value a man for the quality he is of, but for the qualities he possesses. _____

_____

_____

_____

14. Today is yesterday's pupil. _____

_____

_____

15. Old boys have their playthings as well as young ones; the difference is only in the price.

_____

_____

_____

16. Keep your eyes wide open before marriage, half shut afterwards. _____

_____

_____

17. Let our fathers and grandfathers be valued for their goodness, ourselves for our own.

_____

_____

_____

18. The greatest monarch on the proudest throne is obliged to sit upon his own arse.

_____

_____

_____

19. Tim was so learned, that he could name a horse in nine languages; so ignorant, that he bought a cow to ride on. _____

_____

_____

_____

20. No man e'er was glorious, who was not laborious.

_____

21. Kings and bears often worry their keepers.

_____

_____

22. Children and princes often will quarrel for trifles.

_____

_____

Further Directions: Now, on your own or in a small group, develop a description of the new American character, based on Franklin's sayings. How is it different from the "typical" European character?

> **Extra Challenge:**
> Using Franklin as a model, write some sayings of your own that give advice to and express characteristics—good or bad—of students at your school.

Focus on U.S. History:
The Era of Colonization and Settlement

How They Lived

Town and country and frontier. New England, middle colonies, and southern colonies. Each had its way of life. Read some of these descriptions, written by people who lived in these places in colonial times.

Pennsylvania (William Penn, 1683)

[O]f all the many places I have seen in the world, I remember not one better seated; so that it seems to me to have been appointed for a town, whether we regard the rivers, or the conveniency of the coves, docks, and springs, the loftiness and soundness of the land, and the air, held by the people of these parts to be very good. It is advanced within less than a year, to about fourscore houses and cottages, . . . where merchants and handicrafts are following their vocations as fast as they can; while the countrymen are close at their farms. . . .

[Y]our provincial settlement, both within and without the town, for situation and soil, are without exception. . . . By God's blessing the affairs of the society will naturally grow in their reputation and profit.

North Carolina (John Urmstone, 1711)

Workmen are dear and scarce. I have about a dozen acres of clear ground, and the rest woods: in all, 300 acres. Had I servants and money, I might live very comfortably upon it, raise good corn of all sorts, and cattle, without any great labor or charges, . . . but for want [of livestock] shall not make any advantage of my land.

I am forced to work hard with axe, hoe, and spade. I have not a stick to burn for any use but what I cut down with my own hands. . . . Men are generally of all trades, and women the like within their spheres. . . . Men are generally carpenters, joiners, wheelwrights, coopers, butchers, tanners, shoemakers, tallow-chandlers, watermen, and what not; women, soap-makers, starch-makers, dyers, etc.

Boston (Francis Goelet, 1750)

Boston, the metropolis of North America, is accounted the largest town upon the continent, having about three thousand houses in it, about two thirds [of] them wooden framed clapboarded etc. [S]ome of them [are] very spacious buildings which together with their gardens about them cover a great deal [of] ground. The streets are very irregular. The main streets are broad and paved with stone. The cross streets are but narrow, mostly paved. . . . The long wharf . . . is noted the longest in North America being near half an English mile in length and runs direct out. One side . . . is full of warehouses from one end to the other. The Bostoniers build a vast number of vessels for sale. . . . They have but one market which is all built of brick about eighty feet long and arched on both sides, being two stories high. . . . In Boston they are very strict observers of the Sabbath day and in service times no persons are allowed [on] the streets but doctors. If you are found upon the streets and the constables meet you they compel you to go either to church or meeting as you choose.

(continued)

How They Lived (continued)

South Carolina (Eliza Lucas, 1742)

South Carolina is an extensive country near the sea. Most of the settled part of it is upon a flat. . . . It abounds with fine naviga- ble rivers and great quantities of fine timber. The country at a great distance . . . [is] very hilly. The soil in general [is] very fertile. . . . The people in general [are] hospi- table and honest and the better sort add to these a polite, genteel behavior. . . . The winters here are fine and pleasant but four months in the year are extremely disagree- able—excessively hot, [with] much thunder and lightning, and mosquitoes and sand flies in abundance.

Charles Town, the metropolis, is a neat, pretty place. [T]he inhabitants [are] polite and live a very genteel manner. [T]he streets and houses [are] regularly built, the ladies and gentlemen gay in their dress. Upon the whole you will find as many agreeable people of both sexes for the size of the place as almost anywhere. St. Phillips' Church in Charles Town is a very elegant one and much frequented. There are several more places of public worship in the town.

New England (John Adams, 1775)

New England has . . . the advantage of every other colony in America, and, indeed, of every other part of the world that. . . .

1. The people are pure English blood . . . descended from Englishmen . . . who left Europe in purer times than the present, and less tainted with corruption than those they left behind . . .

2. The institutions . . . for the support of religion, morals, and decency exceed any other; obliging every parish to have a minister, and every person to go to meet- ing.

3. The public institutions . . . for the education of youth, supporting colleges at the public expense, and obliging towns to maintain grammar schools, are not equaled . . . in any part of the world.

4. The division of territory . . . into town- ships; empowering towns to assemble, choose officers, make laws, mend roads . . . gives every man an opportunity of showing and improving that education which he received at college or at school.

A Virginia plantation (William Byrd, 1732)

We all kept snug in our several apartments till nine, except Miss Theky, who was the housewife of the family. At that hour we met over a pot of coffee, which was not quite strong enough to give us the palsy. After breakfast the colonel and I left the ladies to their domestic affairs, and took a turn in the garden. . . . I let him understand that besides the pleasure of paying him a visit, I came to be instructed by so great a master in the mystery of making iron, wherein he had led the way. . . . Our conversation on this subject continued till dinner, which was both elegant and plentiful. The afternoon was devoted to the ladies, who showed me one of their most beautiful walks. . . . At night we drank prosperity to all the colonel's projects in a bowl of rack punch, and then retired to our devotions.

Focus on U.S. History:
The Era of Colonization and Settlement

How They Lived: A Group Activity

You have just read several contemporaneous descriptions of colonial life. Those descriptions are an introduction to the following group activity.

Step One:

Your teacher will divide the class into small groups. Each group will investigate social and cultural life in a particular colonial region, city, or town.

Step Two:

Do some research. Read other descriptions of colonial life in your region, city, or town. You can read more descriptions written by people who lived during colonial times, like the ones you just read. You can read portrayals of colonial life written by historians. You can read historical fiction, too. As a group, identify these other sources. Assign different ones to different group members.

Step Three:

After all group members have done their reading, meet again. Discuss what you've learned about life in your region, city, or town. Develop a list of topics to include in a report about everyday colonial life. Some topics to consider are family structure, gender roles, chil-

dren's lives, schooling, housing, daily tasks and occupations, religion, participation in community affairs, standard of living, and amusements.

Step Four:

As a group, prepare a report to present to the class that describes colonial life in your region, city, or town. Different group members can tackle different topics within the report, or you can all work together. Be creative! You could present a skit of a day in the life of a colonial family that illustrates all the topics you want to report on. You could create an audiovisual presentation. Several group members could deliver the report orally, while others display illustrations or other visuals.

Step Five:

After all groups have made their presentations, have a class discussion. Identify things that are similar and different about everyday life in the various regions, cities, or towns. How would you account for these similarities and differences?

The Colonial Economy

The objective of this unit is to build students' understanding of colonial labor systems and colonial economic life. The colonies developed a robust economy, linked to trade. The mercantilist system encouraged colonists to produce what they needed for their basic needs and to export cash crops and raw materials to the mother country, which in turn shipped manufactured goods back to the colonies. Each region adapted its resources to this system, which was further affected by the Navigation Acts. Distinct labor systems evolved to meet the needs of the expanding colonial economy.

Student Activities

Colonial Resources: Mapping visually demonstrates differences in the economic resources of the various colonial regions by having students cut out and position resource symbols on the map of colonial North America.

Colonial Resources: Exports and Imports shows the monetary differences between exports and imports of various colonies. Students create graphs from data supplied on their activity sheet and then add the monetary information to the resources map from the previous activity. Challenge questions ask students to interpret the data.

Mercantilism: Mapping offers more practice in mapping. Students locate major ports and regions in the Atlantic area and trace trade exchanges to discover colonial shipping patterns.

Economic Choices asks students to assume various colonial identities and choose an appropriate business activity for each colonist's region and circumstances. As an extra challenge, students may draw up a detailed business plan for their economic choice.

Colonial Workers presents contemporary descriptions of three types of colonial workers—indentured servant, slave, and transported convict. (You may wish to go over these descriptions in class to be sure that all students understand them.)

Comparing Colonial Workers uses a comparison chart to clarify differences among types of colonial workers. For an extra challenge students can explain the difference between indentured servants and redemptioners.

Runaways underscores how conditions of servitude for slaves and indentured servants alike could become intolerable. Students should be able to understand the advertisements for runaways. Role-playing master, servant, or slave brings the relationships of servitude to life.

The Navigation Acts and You personalizes what might otherwise seem rather dry. Students assume the role of different people in different economic situations to identify how the Navigation Acts affect them personally. The extra challenge activity extends students' knowledge about the Acts and mercantilism by having them create a chart of advantages and disadvantages, to England and to the colonies, and then come to an overall conclusion about how the Navigation Acts affected the colonial economy.

The Colonial Economy

The first settlers in British North America in the early 1600's nearly starved to death at Jamestown and Plymouth during their first winters. By the time of the American Revolution, in 1775, the colonial economy was booming. The white colonial standard of living was among the highest in the world.

> The type of trade practiced in the colonies is called **mercantilism**. England earned more money from exporting more expensive finished goods than it spent on importing cheaper raw materials from its colonies. This means England had a "favorable balance of trade."

Many factors contributed to this economic success. The Americas had abundant natural resources. Land, although it had to be taken from Native Americans, defended, and cleared, seemed limitless. Colonial conditions favored people who were hardworking, ambitious, and independent. A strong market economy soon developed. The colonial population grew rapidly, creating a rich demand for all sorts of goods and services. Overseas markets thirsted for colonial raw materials and resources as well.

The colonies were originally intended as sources of precious metals—gold and silver—for the mother nations. Only Central and South America, colonized by the Spanish, provided these riches. North American profits had to come from trade in other natural resources. British leaders encouraged widespread settlement. Here's how the economic system worked:

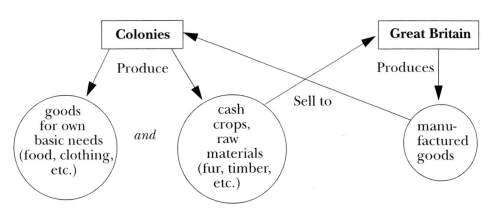

As each colonial region developed, its settlers discovered ways to make the economy thrive. **New England** soil was mostly thin and rocky. Farms could produce food enough for the region, but cash crops for export were mostly out of the question. The fur trade dwindled by the mid-1600's, so New Englanders looked to their other abundant resources, timber and fish, which became profitable exports. Shipping and shipbuilding also were core features of the New England economy.

(continued)

The **middle colonies** had the most diverse population, with people from several nationalities and religions. The economy was also very mixed. Farms blessed with rich tillable soil provided for the needs of the region. They also produced wheat, bread, and flour for export, especially to the slave-holding West Indies. Trade thrived. Artisans' skills were in demand. Producing iron and milling flour were other routes to business success.

The economic success of the **South** was tied to its cash crops. In 1612 John Rolfe had introduced West Indian tobacco to Virginia. The soil and climate were ideal. Tobacco became the mainstay of the Virginia and Maryland economies, as well as an important part of North Carolina's. In South Carolina, rice production began in the 1690's in the flat, low coastal areas. In the 1740's Eliza Lucas introduced indigo, which grows on higher ground, as another cash export crop. Georgia remained mostly a frontier area, grounded in subsistence farming.

Labor Systems

The expanding colonial economy constantly demanded more and more labor—workers. Natural population increases alone couldn't meet the demand.

- As you learned in Unit 1, **indentured servants** provided a lot of this labor in the 1600's.
- **Convicts** who were transported to the colonies often had to sign for some years of service.
- **Free immigrants** and indentured servants supplied most of the extra labor needs of the northern and middle colonies.
- The growing plantation system in the South, however, required great amounts of labor. Black **slaves** provided most of it.

(Black slaves also worked in the North, but not nearly so many as in the South. Unit 7 has more background about the development of slavery.)

The Navigation Acts

England wanted the colonial trade to benefit the mother country first. The colonies, as part of the British Empire, could also benefit, but in second place. Only then could foreign nations enter the trade picture.

Parliament wanted to regulate some aspects of colonial trade. To do this, it passed a series of laws called the Navigation Acts, beginning in 1650.

- Foreign ships were barred from the colonies.
- Colonial imports and exports had to be carried only in British or colonial ships.
- Products from Europe had to be unloaded and reloaded in England before they could go on to the colonies.
- Certain "enumerated" colonial products could only be shipped within the British Empire. In 1660 these included sugar, tobacco, cotton, indigo, and ginger. Later, rice, molasses, furs, copper, and naval stores (pitch, tar, turpentine, etc.) were also enumerated.

Until the 1760's, British restrictions on colonial trade weren't very troublesome. Many important trade items were never enumerated. Colonists could sell fish, corn, and wheat, for example, to any foreign nation that wanted them. Also, colonial merchants tended to ignore laws they didn't like. Enforcement was spotty. Customs officials were regularly bribed. Smuggling was common. When Britain tried to enforce the trade laws and impose stricter ones, in the 1760's, revolutionary unrest began simmering.

Colonial Resources: Mapping

Directions: Each region of colonial North America contributed to the robust colonial economy in its own way. Identify the resources, products, and commercial activities of each region. First, cut out the symbols on this page. Then, place each one appropriately on the map of colonial North America.

beaver

indigo

timber and lumber products

naval stores (tar, pitch, turpentine)

fish

iron

rum distilling

small manufacturing

shipbuilding

small subsistence farming

tobacco

large farming

grains, flour

large plantations

rice

small cash crops

New England became a hub of the **"triangular trade."** Merchants from the region purchased molasses in the West Indies, distilled it into rum back in New England, traded the rum in Africa for black slaves, sold the slaves in the West Indies, and then purchased more molasses. . . . Do you see why this was triangular? (If not, check it out on the map of the Atlantic region.)

Colonial Resources: Exports and Imports

Imports are things shipped *into* a country or colony. **Exports** are things sent *out* of a country or colony. People in the colonies earned money by selling overseas things they produced. England earned money by selling items it produced to people in the colonies.

Directions: Use these figures on the economies of the colonies to do two things.

1. Create a bar graph showing the differences in the values of exports and imports for different colonies/regions.

2. Add these figures to your colonial resources map.

Average Value of Exports to and Imports from England by American Colonies Period from 1751–1755 (in pounds sterling)					
	Exports	**Imports**		**Exports**	**Imports**
New England	£ 69,415	£ 319,215	Virginia and Maryland	£545,045	£327,525
New York	£ 37,655	£ 199,880	Carolinas	£270,230	£167,820
Pennsylvania	£ 31,070	£ 205,465	Georgia	£ 2,560	£ 4,790
Totals (all)	£955,975	£1,224,695			

Challenge Questions:

1. Which colony or region spent the most on imported English goods? _____

   Why might this be so? _____

   _____

2. Which colony or region sold the most to England? _____

   Why might this be so? _____

   _____

3. Overall, does it seem as if trade with the colonies was profitable for England? _____

   Explain your answer: _____

   _____

Mercantilism: Mapping

Directions: Use the map of the Atlantic region.

1. Locate and label these major ports and regions in the North American and Caribbean colonies, Europe, and Africa.

Ivory Coast	London	New York	Philadelphia
Gold Coast	Bristol	Boston	Charles Town
Slave Coast	Glasgow	West Indies	Lisbon

2. Draw shipping lines showing the triangular or two-way trading exchanges listed below. Label each leg of the trade exchange with the goods being carried on that leg.

fish ⟶ wine, fruit ⟶ manufactured goods ⟶
>

rice, indigo ⟶ manufactured goods ⟶ >

wheat, flour ⟶ sugar ⟶ manufactured goods ⟶ >

rum ⟶ slaves ⟶ molasses, sugar ⟶ >

tobacco ⟶ manufactured goods ⟶
>

lumber ⟶ manufactured goods ⟶ >

Economic Choices

The colonies were a land of opportunity. People who came there or were born and grew up there looked for, and found, many ways to make a good living. The type of business a person chose to engage in depended partly on local and regional conditions and resources.

Directions: Read the following descriptions. Then tell about the type of business you'd go into in each case. Be sure to explain why your business activity is a good choice for that area.

1. You live along the James River in Virginia. You own 300 acres of fertile land.

2. You live in Newport, Rhode Island, a busy port city of New England.

3. You (like Benjamin Franklin) have just arrived in Philadelphia in 1723.

4. You live in upstate New York, near Albany and the Hudson River. Your area abounds in timber and fur resources.

5. You have just arrived in Charles Town, South Carolina. It's a bustling port, with a sophisticated social life. You have inherited 400 acres of excellent low-lying coastal farmland. You own an additional 200 acres of high ground.

6. You are a Scotch-Irish emigrant to the backcountry of the Chesapeake colonies. You live in the foothills of the Appalachian Mountains, beyond navigable rivers.

Extra Challenge: Draw up a detailed plan for the business activity you intend to pursue.

Focus on U.S. History:
The Era of Colonization and Settlement

Name _____

Date _____

Colonial Workers

In order for the colonial economy to grow and thrive, the colonies needed lots of workers. Some were native-born colonists. Others were free immigrants. Many more, though, were black African slaves and indentured European servants. Some were convicts sent over to get them out of England. To understand more about colonial workers, read these descriptions.

Document of Indenture

THIS INDENTURE WITNESSES that we, the Overseers of the Poor of the City of London, do place and bond out **Martha Williams**, now in the Alms house, unto **James Samuels**, of the City of Boston in the colony of Massachusetts. The said Martha Williams is to dwell and serve with the said James Samuels from this date of October 5, 1701, until the full term of five years be completed and ended on October 4, 1706. During all of this term, the said Williams shall faithfully serve her said master and gladly obey his lawful commands everywhere. She shall not commit fornication nor contract matrimony within the said term.

The said master, during the said term of service, shall teach the said servant to read, write, and cipher, and shall also teach her all branches of good housewifery. He shall find and provide for the said servant sufficient and wholesome meat, drink, clothing, lodging, and washing fit for a servant during all the said term. At the end of said term, the master shall give the servant two good suits of wearing apparel.

Virginia Slave Law, 1669

Be it enacted and declared, if any slave resists his master and by the extremity of the correction should chance to die, that his death shall not be accounted a felony. The master [must] be acquitted from molestation, since it cannot be presumed that premeditated malice (which alone makes murder a felony) should induce any man to destroy his own estate [property].

On Transported Convicts, by William Eddis, 1770

Persons convicted of felony, and in consequence transported to this continent, if they are able to pay the expense of passage, are free to pursue their fortune agreeably to their inclinations or abilities. Few, however, have means to avail themselves of this advantage. These unhappy beings are, generally, consigned to an agent, who classes them suitably to their real or supposed qualifications; advertises them for sale; and disposes of them, for seven years, to planters, to mechanics, and to such as choose to retain them for domestic service.

Focus on U.S. History:
The Era of Colonization and Settlement

Name _____

Date _____

Comparing Colonial Workers

Directions: From what you have read on the previous page, fill in this chart about the differences among different types of colonial workers.

Type of Worker	Terms of Work/Service	Why They Came to the Colonies	Advantages and Disadvantages of Being This Type of Worker
Indentured Servant			
Slave			
Transported Convict			
Free Immigrant or Native Colonist			

Extra Challenge:

There was a technical difference between immigrants who came to the colonies as **indentured servants** and as **redemptioners**. Explain this difference. Were the terms and conditions of service for these two types of workers very different in reality?

Focus on U.S. History:
The Era of Colonization and Settlement

Runaways

The life of a slave or an indentured servant could be miserable. Even if a slave was treated well, he or she could yearn strongly for freedom. So ads for runaway slaves and servants were common in colonial newspapers. Here are a few.

RUN AWAY from Marten Ryerson, of Readingtown, a young servant man named *William Hains*, small stature, ruddy complexion, big nose, big blue eyes, pock-broken, had no hair, branded on the brawn of his thumb, of the left hand. Had on when he run away a white shirt, and a sailor's frock, a pair of trousers, but has since got a Greek vestment. It's probable that he has changed his name, for he has already passed by the name of *Thomson* and *Robinson*. Whoever takes up the said servant, and secures him so that his said master may have him again, shall have *five pounds* reward besides all reasonable charges paid by

MARTIN RYERSON.

RUN AWAY from Nicholas Bearcraft of Hunterdon County, a black wench, named *Hecatissa* alias *Savina*, country born, about 27 years of age, short stature, gloomy down look, often troubled with the colic. It is thought she may be gone towards Maryland. Whoever takes up and secures said wench, so that she may be had again, shall have *twenty shillings* reward, and reasonable charges, paid by

NICHOLAS BEARCRAFT.

TAKEN UP, about six months ago, as a runaway, and now is in Trenton jail, one *John Parra*, a well-set fellow, about 24 years of age, and pretends to know something of the hatter's trade. If no person claims him before the first day of May next, he will be sold for defraying his charges. *By Order of the Court.*

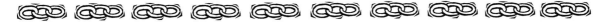

Directions: Consider the reasons that may have prompted John, Hecatissa, or William to run away. Think about the master's reaction. Then, with classmates, role-play a hearing in which

• the runaway explains his or her actions and

• the master responds, giving reasons why the runaway must be returned to service or slavery.

• The hearing officer could be impartial, an antislavery Quaker, or a servant-owning employer, and so on. Witnesses could also speak at the hearing.

The Navigation Acts and You

Directions: In the Student Background Pages, you read about the Navigation Acts. England used these acts to try to control colonial trade to its advantage. Imagine you are each of the colonial businesspeople listed below. How do the Navigation Acts affect you?

1. You are a Virginia tobacco grower.

2. You own a shipbuilding company in Maine.

3. You and your husband have a thriving wheat farm in Delaware. Your son and his wife operate a busy flour mill.

4. You own a rice plantation in South Carolina.

5. You and your brother fish for cod off the coast of New England.

6. Your southern plantation produces indigo.

7. You want to purchase casks of French wine for your Richmond hotel.

8. You produce rum from molasses you buy in the West Indies.

Extra Challenge: Create a chart of advantages and disadvantages of mercantilism and the Navigation Acts on England and the colonies. Did the Acts hamper the colonial economy in a significant way?

The Rise of Slavery

The objective of this unit is for students to understand how slavery developed in colonial North America. Europeans discovered African slavery in the 1400's. Growth of large plantations in the Caribbean and in the southern colonies of North America fueled a large demand for labor in the 1700's, and the African slave trade boomed. How slaves were treated varied among regions. Forced into a new life far from their homes, families, and cultures, African slaves evolved a new African-American culture that incorporated elements of their shared African past. They also resisted their condition, sometimes overtly, with violence, but more often in subtler but effective ways.

Student Activities

Mapping the Slave Trade has students identify slave origins and slave destinations on the Atlantic region map and draw trade lines to connect them. Questions lead students to realize that only a small percentage of African slaves came to British North America (and to the new United States). For an extra challenge, students can graph the slave importation data.

Graphing the Slave Trade uses a bar graph to compare numbers of slaves exported from Africa, by exporting country, for various blocks of time.

Reading the Slave Trade Graph helps students interpret information in the graph to learn more about the slave trade and the nations who participated in it.

The Middle Passage presents first-person descriptions of slave-ship journeys from Africa across the Atlantic. (You might want to go over these in class to be sure all students understand them.)

In **Describing the Middle Passage** students use the material they have just read to imagine themselves aboard a slave ship and describe the experience from the point of view of various people on the voyage. The extra challenge activity has students role-play discussion among the people on board, justifying and arguing against the slave trade.

African-American Culture gives students a frame to identify elements of African culture that the captives retained when they were forced to evolve a new American slave culture. For an extra challenge, students identify African contributions to American agriculture in the colonial period.

Time Line: Slavery presents important events in the history of slavery in North America. Students date each event and add it to their time line.

The Rise of Slavery

As you learned in Unit 5, the American colonies needed laborers to work the land. Indentured servants helped, but the demand was much greater than the supply. European shipmasters trading in Africa discovered a rich new source of labor: black slaves. For centuries it had been common practice in Africa to enslave prisoners of war. These enslaved prisoners often became members of their new families and communities. Some Africans also became slaves in order to pay their debts. Others were sentenced to slavery as the penalty for adultery.

The Slave Trade

Portuguese traders began buying African slaves in the 1400's. Other European nations soon joined in this profitable commerce. African rulers strictly controlled the trade. Europeans were permitted only to rent land for trading forts at certain sites along the coast. The Africans themselves captured prisoners in the interior areas. The African slavers drove their captives to the coastal forts, where they delivered them to the European slavers in exchange for rum, trade goods, and guns and ammunition. The slave trade badly disrupted life in West Africa, creating constant chaos and violence.

> Traders drove their captured African slaves to the coast in **coffles**—trains of people fastened together. Male slaves were tied by the neck to a long wooden pole, which they dragged along, or two men would be tied by the neck to a single pole, one man at each end. This made escape impossible. Drivers would whip the exhausted slaves along to force a good pace.

Many captured Africans did not survive their forced relocation. Some died during the initial raid. Others fell during the trek to the coast. Worst of all was the voyage across the Atlantic. Deaths occurred from disease, suffocation, suicide, rebellion, starvation, and brutality. Illegal slavers about to be arrested sometimes practiced mass murder by throwing their captives overboard at sea.

Slavery in the Americas

Some African slaves came to Spanish America in the 1500's. Several were in Virginia with Spaniards in 1526. The first known black Africans in British North America arrived in 1619. A Dutch ship brought these 20 captives to Jamestown, Virginia.

At first, blacks in the British colonies may have been treated as indentured servants. But the demand for labor, especially on southern plantations, increased. Tobacco and rice plantations needed many workers. Sugar plantations in the Caribbean needed many more. Slavery seemed to be the perfect solution (for the slaveholder!). Here's why:

Indentured Servant	Slave
Bound for set number of years	Bound for life
Children are free—not bound	Children are slaves—bound for life
Escape easy—white skin, blends in	Escape hard—black skin, easily noticed

(continued)

European prejudices certainly played a role in the growth of black slavery in the Americas. Europeans thought all "heathens" were inferior. Such people could only benefit from being owned by Christians. Also, Europeans linked blackness with the devil, with dirt, with fearful and threatening darkness. Gradually, slavery became legally established in the colonies. Virginia declared its African slaves "perpetual servants" in 1662. Maryland enacted a similar law in 1664.

The conditions of slave life varied, by slave owner and by region. Here's how:

Brazil:	Spanish West Indies:	French West Indies:
Male slaves have many chances to become free. Race mixing common. Social levels open.	Law gives slaves some rights. Male slaves can buy their own freedom and their children's freedom.	Laws control treatment of slaves, but laws are often ignored.

Dutch West Indies:	British West Indies/British North America:	
Slaves are generally treated harshly.	Few slaves become free. Slaves are chattel—property, objects, not people with rights. Owner's power over slave is total.	

Black Resistance

Blacks, of course, bitterly objected to being slaves. But they had few ways to resist in the North American colonies. An African suddenly placed in an alien society and an alien culture couldn't run away. Where would he go? Who would help her? Blacks not on their owner's plantation would always be spotted because of their skin color. Failure to obey a master's or overseer's orders would result in brutal beatings.

Still, some slaves did rebel. Here are some examples:

- About 25 black slaves set a fire in New York City in 1712. Then, as planned, they killed some of the whites who tried to put out the fire.

- About 100 slaves attacked whites and fled toward Florida in South Carolina's Stono rebellion of 1739. They were defeated in a fierce battle against white militia and Indians.

- Other serious rebellions occurred later in the 1700's and the 1800's. (You'll learn more about them in Book 4 of this series.)

Also, slaves practiced subtler forms of resistance. They performed acts of sabotage—digging up crop seedlings while hoeing weeds, for example, or damaging farm equipment. They pilfered many items, insisting that what belonged to the plantation owner belonged to them as well. They pretended to be too dull-witted to do their tasks correctly. They worked as slowly as possible. They committed many acts of arson.

TO BE SOLD *by* **William** Yeomans, (in *Charles Town* Merchant,) a parcel of good Plantation Slaves. Encouragement will be given by taking Rice in Payment, or any leg faddles and Furniture, choice Barbados and Boston Rum, also Cordial Waters and Limejuice, as well as a parcel of extraordinary Indian trading Goods, and many of other forts fuitable for the Seafon. a Time Credit, Security to be given if required There's likewife to be fold, very good Troopling

Ad in the *Charlestown Gazette*, mid 1600's

(continued)

Focus on U.S. History:
The Era of Colonization and Settlement

African-American Culture

Through all this, enslaved blacks added elements of their African culture to the new slave culture they were forced to evolve. Africans imported into the Americas came from different backgrounds and spoke many different languages. The condition of being black in white America was what created a sense among slaves of being "African." They also shared many broad cultural traditions, which gave them a further feeling of being bonded as Africans.

Religion, with traditional African spirits and gods mixing with the Christianity of the new culture, was part of everyday life. Their prayerful response to a constant spiritual presence was lively—singing, dancing, shouting. African culture also placed high value on the family and the community. Because of this, black slaves preferred to work together, in groups rather than individually. They made up songs about work and religious beliefs (and rebellious thoughts) that were sung in a call-and-response group style. Ripped from their original families, slaves formed new ones. Many owners tried to avoid breaking up these strong families because the affected slaves would quickly become poor workers in revenge.

African slaves also brought their folk medicines and charms with them to the Americas. These included love potions—and poison, another often-used weapon against white owners. African folk art was kept alive in wood carvings, quilts, baskets, mats, and the like. By holding on to some African traditions, black slaves in America kept part of their African identity.

African-American slaves often sang in a **call-and-response** style. A leader sings a line. The other group members sing a line of response. Then the leader sings the next line, and the group sings its response, and so on. Here's an example from the spiritual "O, Wasn't That a Wide River."

Leader: O, the river of Jordan is so wide,

Response: One more river to cross,

Leader: I don't know how to get on the other side,

Response: One more river to cross.

Leader: Satan is just a snake in the grass,

Response: One more river to cross,

Leader: If you ain't mighty careful he will hold you fast,

Response: One more river to cross.

Focus on U.S. History:
The Era of Colonization and Settlement

Mapping the Slave Trade

List 1	List 2	
African Origins of North American Slaves (listed in order, from source of largest number of slaves down to source of smallest number)	**Slaves Imported into the Americas, 1451–1870** (estimated)*	
	Region or Country	**Number**
Angola	Brazil	4,190,000
Bight of Biafra	British Caribbean	2,443,000
Gold Coast	Spanish America	1,687,000
Senegambia	French Caribbean	1,655,000
Windward Coast	British North America	
Sierra Leone	and United States	523,000
Bight of Benin	Dutch Caribbean	500,000
Mozambique-Madagascar	Danish Caribbean	50,000

Directions

1. On the map of the Atlantic region, locate and label the places in Africa that North American slaves came from. (Use the List 1 information. One of the listed places is off the map. Indicate with an arrow where it would be found.)

2. Then, locate the places in North America where those slaves were taken. Use color-coding to show these different regions. (Use the List 2 information.)

3. Draw lines from West Africa to each slave-importing region named in List 2. On each line, write the total number of slaves imported to that region.

   a. Which region or country imported the most slaves? _____

   b. How many slaves were imported to British North America and the United States?
   _____

   c. How many slaves were imported to other parts of the Americas? _____

4. Why isn't Brazil included in "Spanish America" in List 2? _____

_____

Extra Challenge: On a piece of graph paper, construct a bar or line graph of the information in List 2.

*Figures from James A. Rawley, *The Transatlantic Slave Trade: A History* (New York: W.W. Norton, 1981).

Graphing the Slave Trade

Numbers of Slaves Exported from Africa, by Exporting Country*

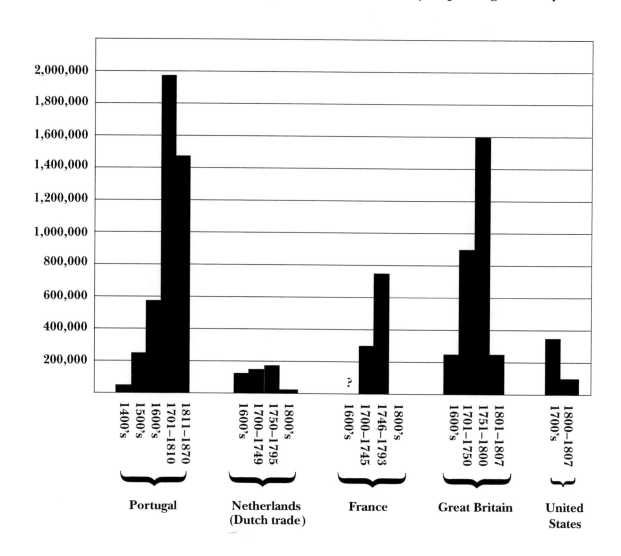

Note: Some figures are unknown, so are not shown here. Total numbers of African slaves imported into the Americas probably are around 10 to 11 million.

*Figures from James A. Rawley, *The Transatlantic Slave Trade: A History* (New York: W.W. Norton, 1981).

Reading the Slave Trade Graph

Directions: Use the slave trade graph on page 86 that shows numbers of African slaves imported into the Americas to answer these questions.

Slave auction

1. Which country's ships carried the most slaves to the Americas during the years of the slave trade?

   _____

2. Which country's ships carried the second highest number of slaves to the Americas during the years of the slave trade? _____

3. Which two countries' ships carried the fewest slaves to the Americas during the years of the slave trade? _____

4. ApproximatelyhowmanyslavesdidshipsfromthecoloniesbringtotheAmericasduringthe 1700's?

5. During what years did Great Britain's ships bring more than a million slaves to the Americas?

6. According to the bar graph, Portugal's ships imported more than a million slaves to the Americas during two periods. Identify these periods, and give the approximate number of slaves imported during each period.

   Time span (years): _____ Number of slaves imported: _____

   Time span (years): _____ Number of slaves imported: _____

7. In all, about how many slaves were imported to the Americas from Africa during the 1700's?

   _____

8. Which country's ships imported the vast majority of slaves during the 1800's?

   _____

   Why did the other countries' ships stop importing African slaves during the 1800's?

   _____

   _____

Focus on U.S. History:
The Era of Colonization and Settlement

The Middle Passage

The journey of the slave ships from Africa to the Americas was called the Middle Passage. For African slaves it was a journey of despair and danger. Torn from their homes, chained slaves endured overcrowding, brutality, filth and stench, and life-threatening disease. Their response was often depression, revolt, or suicide. Read these eyewitness accounts.

Olaudah Euqiana (Gustavus Vassa), an Ibo captured as a child:

When I looked round the ship . . . and saw a large furnace or copper boiling, and a multitude of black people of every description chained together, every one of their countenances expressing dejection and sorrow, I no longer doubted of my fate; and, quite overpowered with horror and anguish, I fell motionless on the deck and fainted.

I was soon put down under the decks, and there I received such a salutation in my nostrils as I had never experienced in my life: so that with the loathsomeness of the stench and crying together, I became so sick and low that I was not able to eat, nor had I the least desire to taste anything.

I now wished for the last friend, death, to relieve me; but soon, to my grief, two of the white men offered me eatables; and, on my refusing to eat, one of them held me fast by the hands, and laid me across, I think, the windlass, and tied my feet, while the other flogged me severely.

But still I feared I should be put to death, the white people looked and acted, as I thought, in so savage a manner; for I had never seen among any people such instances of brutal cruelty; and this not only shown towards us blacks, but also to some of the whites themselves.

The closeness of the place, and the heat of the climate, added to the number in the ship, which was so crowded that each had scarcely room to turn himself, almost suffocated us. This produced copious perspirations, so that the air soon became unfit for respiration, from a variety of loathsome smells, and brought on a sickness among the slaves, of which many died. . . .

Many a time we were near suffocation from the want of fresh air, which we were often without for whole days together. This, and the stench of the necessary tubs, carried off many.

(continued)

Focus on U.S. History:
The Era of Colonization and Settlement

The Middle Passage *(continued)*

Thomas Phillip, captain of the ship *Hannibal,* 1693 voyage

The Negroes are so loth to leave their own country, that they have often leaped out of the canoes, boat and ship, into the sea, and kept under water till they were drowned, to avoid being taken up and saved by our boats, which pursued them. . . . We had about 12 Negroes did willfully drown themselves, and others starved themselves to death; for tis their belief that when they die they return home to their own country and friends again.

When our slaves are aboard we shackle the men two and two, while we lie in port, and in sight of their own country, for tis then they attempt to make their escape and mutiny. . . . When we come to sea we let them all out of irons, they never then attempting to rebel, considering that should they kill or master us, they could not tell how to manage the ship.

No gold-finders can endure so much noisome slavery as they do who carry Negroes; . . . we endure twice the misery; and yet by their [the slaves'] mortality [dying] our voyages are ruined, and we pine and fret ourselves to death, to think that we should undergo so much misery, and take so much pains to so little purpose [profit].

Surgeon's mate, the *Ruby,* 1790 testimony to Parliament

Not infrequently, after slaves were brought on board, they would refuse to eat and the captain would order them flogged unmercifully until they obeyed, in fact, he usually plied the cat on the naked backs of the blacks and seemed to find a pleasant sensation in the sight of blood and the sound of their moans.

If the sea was rough the slaves were unable to dance and whenever it rained hard they were kept below, and the gratings were covered with tarpaulins which made it very hot below and nearly suffocated the slaves. . . . Dysentery usually followed a spell of bad weather and the mucus and filth among the slaves below made the slave deck a horrible place.

(continued)

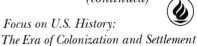

The Middle Passage *(continued)*

A ship's doctor's account, published in 1788

The men, on being brought aboard ship, are immediately fastened together, two and two, by handcuffs on their wrists and by irons rivetted on their legs. They are then sent down between the decks. . . . They are frequently stowed so close as to admit of no other position than lying on their sides. Nor will the height between decks . . . allow them to stand. . . . The tubs [for "bathroom" purposes] are much too small for the purpose intended and usually are emptied but once every day. . . . As the necessities of nature are not to be resisted, [slaves who can't reach the tubs] ease themselves as they lie.

Exercise being considered necessary for the preservation of their health they are sometimes obliged to dance when the weather will permit their coming on deck. If they go about it reluctantly or do not move with agility, they are flogged; a person standing by them all the time with a cat-o'-nine-tails in his hand for that purpose.

The fresh air being excluded, the Negroes' rooms very soon grow intolerably hot. The confined air, rendered noxious by the effluvia exhaled from their bodies and by being repeatedly breathed, soon produces fevers and fluxes which generally carry off great numbers of them. . . . The floor of their rooms was so covered with the blood and mucus which had proceeded from them in consequence of the flux, that it resembled a slaughter-house. It is not in the power of the human imagination to picture a situation more dreadful or disgusting.

Slave trader, voyage of 1808

The day before we were to start, the branding was done and a good deal of flogging had to be done also to keep the frightened Negroes quiet. Shakoe's lash and the heavy whips of his assistant Negroes were not idle for a moment. The slaves were fetched up singly, made to lie down on their faces where they are held by a big Negro while another kept the branding irons hot in a fire close by and a third applied them between the shoulders of the shrieking wretches.

90   *Focus on U.S. History:*
                                                        The Era of Colonization and Settlement

Describing the Middle Passage

Directions: Be sure you have read the descriptions of the Middle Passage on the previous pages. Then write a paragraph describing a Middle Passage voyage from each of these points of view.

1. A white sailor

2. A female slave, age 16

3. A cabin boy, age 10

4. The ship's captain

5. The ship's doctor or a passenger

6. A male slave, age 24

Extra Challenge: With classmates, role-play people aboard the slave ship who are justifying and arguing against the slave trade.

Focus on U.S. History:
The Era of Colonization and Settlement

African-American Culture

Slave owners didn't want their African slaves to keep their native cultures. A black slave stripped of his or her identity as an African had only one identity left: slave. The captives outwardly adopted the new culture. But they added African elements to it.

Directions: From what you have read, identify elements of African culture in the following.

1. **Religion:** Africans taught about Christianity were told to be meek, obedient, and submissive—it was God's will for them to be slaves.

   Africans' response: _____

   _____

   _____

2. **Music:** Slaves were not encouraged to express themselves with African music.

   Africans' response: _____

   _____

   _____

3. **Family structure:** Owners could ignore family ties, sell a husband, a wife, or children.

   Africans' response: _____

   _____

   _____

4. **Literacy (reading and writing):** It was against the law to teach a slave how to read and write.

   Africans' response: _____

   _____

   _____

5. **Language:** Slaves were forbidden to speak their native African tongues.

   Africans' response: _____

   _____

   _____

Extra Challenge: Africans introduced some important things to American agriculture, especially in the Carolinas. Identify West African contributions in these areas:

(a) crops: _____

_____

(b) animal raising: _____

_____

(c) fishing: _____

_____

Time Line: Slavery

Directions: With classmates, construct a time line of these important events in the history of slavery in North America or add them to your ongoing time line. (Hint: Events are listed in the order in which they occurred.)

A Dutch ship brings 20 blacks to Jamestown, Virginia

Dutch West Indies Company founded

Dutch take over Portuguese slave trade

Virginia law: children born of a slave woman are slaves; African slaves are "perpetual servants"

Plot to rebel discovered among black slaves and white indentured servants in Virginia

Virginia law: slaves who are baptized as Christians remain slaves

Slave revolt in Jamaica

Virginia law: a master who kills a slave he is punishing for resistance of any kind faces no legal penalty

Virginia slave plot exposed; leaders executed

New York City slave revolt; about 25 blacks, some whites killed

Almost yearly, slave revolts in Jamaica

Guianas revolt (approximately 18 revolts from this date to end of slavery)

Stono, South Carolina, rebellion; about 100 slaves defeated in hard battle with militia, Indians

New York plot foiled; over 100 accused

Slave plot to capture Annapolis, Maryland

South Carolina law: death penalty to slaves who try to poison whites

Tacky's rebellion in Jamaica, about 1,000 slaves

Focus on U.S. History:
The Era of Colonization and Settlement

ANSWER KEY
ADDITIONAL ACTIVITIES
ASSESSMENTS

Unit 1: The Early Colonists

Mapping the Spread of European Settlement (page 5)

St. Augustine, 1565, Spanish

Roanoke, 1585, 1587, English

Port Royal, Nova Scotia, 1604, French

Jamestown, 1607, English

Quebec, 1608, French

Fort Nassau (Albany), 1614, Dutch

Plymouth, 1620, English

New Amsterdam (New York), 1624, Dutch

Boston, Massachusetts Bay Colony, 1630, English

St. Mary's, Maryland Colony, 1634, English

Providence, 1636, English

Hartford, 1636, English

Fort Christiana, New Sweden, 1638, Swedish

New Haven, 1638, English

New London, 1646, English

New Jersey Colony, 1665, English

Charles Town, South Carolina, 1670, English

New Hampshire Colony, 1679, English

Philadelphia, Pennsylvania Colony, 1681, English

Germantown, Pennsylvania, 1683, Germans in English colony

Delaware (separate assembly established), 1703, English

New Orleans, 1718, French

Baltimore, 1729, English

Georgia Colony, 1732, English

Challenge Question answer: Most were located on a waterway.

Reading the Immigration Pie Charts (page 7)

1. Massachusetts, New York, South Carolina

2. Massachusetts, South Carolina

3. Pennsylvania; founded as a haven for people of all religions

4. Dutch; New York was originally a Dutch colony

5. Pennsylvania

6. Scotch and Irish

Extra Challenge sample answers:

    a. New England: Most people of similar ethnic background, so culture throughout New England was similar.

    b. Ethnically diverse population, so a diverse culture and practice of many religious faiths.

    c. Heavily English (especially in coastal plantation areas); Scotch and Irish in back-country. A split between the two cultures.

Would You Emigrate? (page 9)

Factors that might motivate each person to emigrate:

1. A desire to spread Christianity among the Native Americans.

2. You fought against the king of England; he will pardon you if you agree to emigrate to North America.

3. This would be your best chance to escape from poverty and lifelong spinsterhood.

4. The Anglican Church is becoming more and more intolerant of your views.

5. You are persecuted in France for your religious beliefs.

6. Cromwell's followers are retaliating against the royalists.

7. Tenants are being kicked off their farms as the land is converted to sheep grazing pasture. You have few economic choices now.

8. New Netherland enjoys a thriving trade; you can do well here.

9. You can't inherit your father's estate; it will all go to your oldest brother. In America, you can put together your own estate.

Note: If students can't find information on religious reasons for emigrating in their textbooks, refer them to the student background pages of Unit 4 in this book.

Those Who Came to the Colonies (page 10)

Types of early colonists:

children—poor, orphan, delinquent

adventurers, traders

unmarried women—poor, or simply single

convicts, felons

vagrants

political dissidents

indentured servants

kidnapping victims

religious dissidents

Come to the Colonies! (page 13)

1. The Native Americans did not become an important market for manufactured English clothing.

2. The much-hoped-for passage to the Spice Islands and the Far East through North America did not exist.

3. The colonists and traders who came to North America did not find treasures of pearls, gold, silver, and precious stones.

4. In spite of attempts at producing the items named, only the dye indigo could be successfully and economically produced in the southern colonies.

5. Virginia was not a suitable place for gold or silver mining. The early colonists needed to plant, fish, erect buildings, etc., not spend their time looking for precious metals. The Virginia investors never made profits from these metals.

Additional Activity Suggestions

Students could do any of the following activities.

1. Visit Plimoth Plantation or Jamestown. Share your visit with classmates via an oral report and photographs.

2. Create a model of the Jamestown or Plymouth settlement.

3. Read Longfellow's poem "The Courtship of Miles Standish," which is set in the Plymouth settlement. Then do research to find out the actual historical facts about the story.

4. Write a description, perhaps in diary form, of your experiences as a European colonist in the first year of an early North American settlement (Jamestown, Plymouth, St. Augustine, Port Royal, Quebec, New Amsterdam, Fort Orange, Fort Christiana, etc.). Then compare your experiences with those of classmates in other settlements.

5. Read actual and fictional accounts of life in various early colonies. See the Resources section for suggestions. Higher-level students could read portions of William Bradford's *Of Plymouth Plantation 1620–1647,* a firsthand account of events by the colony's governor, or of Captain John Smith's *A True Relation . . . of Virginia.*

6. Identify reasons why people emigrate to the United States today. What reasons do they share with the early emigrants to the colonies?

Unit 1 Assessment

Describe your experience as an English emigrant to North America. Why and when did you leave England? What is your status as an immigrant (indentured servant, transported convict, member of a family, adventurer, trader, religious dissident, etc.)? What is your journey across the Atlantic Ocean like? What are your plans for your new life? Where in North America do you land? What do you find there? Is it what you expected? Are you glad you came?

Unit 2: Colonial Conflicts and Native Americans

French and British Wars (page 19)

1. King William's War (1689–1697)

   French and British: At war's end, all captured territory went back to its original owners.

2. Queen Anne's War (1702–1713)

   French: Yielded Nova Scotia, Newfoundland, and Hudson Bay area to Great Britain.

   British: Gained above areas.

3. King George's War (1740–1748)

   French: Got Louisburg back.

   British: Had to give Louisburg back after capturing it.

4. French and Indian War (1754–1763)

   French: Gave up all claims to North America except for two small Canadian islands.

   British: Gained control of all of Canada and the American territories east of the Mississippi River.

Mutual Influences—The Columbian Exchange (page 20)

1. Language

   Native Americans: Some learned to speak English
   Europeans: Adopted many Native American place names, names for native flora and fauna (skunk, moose, raccoon, squash, pecan), and names for Indian artifacts and foods (moccasin, tomahawk, canoe, succotash)

2. Clothing and coverings

   Native Americans: Woolen and cotton garments, blankets
   Europeans: Moccasins, leggings, use of animal pelts for warm clothing

3. Farming

   Native Americans: Use of metal implements
   Europeans: Girdling trees to clear forests; corn and squash culture

4. Health

   Native Americans: Deadly European diseases for which they had no immunity
   Europeans: No new diseases from Native Americans; learned medicinal uses of North American plants

5. Weapons and warfare

   Native Americans: Guns and ammunition
   Europeans: Learned Indians' guerrilla warfare techniques; use of hatchets and tomahawks

6. Food and drink

   Native Americans: Alcoholic beverages; iron pots for cooking
   Europeans: Indian foods, especially corn dishes (hominy, pone, succotash), squash, yams

7. Commerce and ways to travel

   Native Americans: Developed extensive fur trade; economy no longer subsistence
   Europeans: Learned to travel on snowshoes, by canoe

8. Tools

   Native Americans: Metal tools, knives, axes

Living Together: Europeans and Native Americans (page 22)

Predictions will vary. Outcomes follow.

Massachusetts—Plymouth Colony made a peace treaty with Massasoit, chief of the Wampanoags, in 1621. The peace lasted for 20 years. However, tensions did exist, as suggested by Bradford's phrase "savage and brutish men" and Winslow's comment about the Indians having "a fear of us." These tensions would result in the bloody King Philip's War from 1675–1676.

Pennsylvania—This colony was notable for the peaceful relations between colonists and Native Americans. The Indians liked and trusted Penn, who had treated them well and paid them fairly for their lands, by the standards of that time. Because they didn't have to worry about attack, settlers were able to establish large farms in the countryside. The colony prospered. Trouble did break out on the western frontier, though, when the contentious Scotch-Irish began settling there and taking land from the Native Americans.

Virginia—The colony had spotty relations with the Native Americans. At times, they were willing to trade with the settlers. At other times, they attacked. John Smith had a healthy respect for the natives. In 1622 the Indians attacked and massacred many Jamestown settlers. Attacks and counterattacks raged for years afterward.

Challenge Question answer: An epidemic of smallpox had killed many of New England's Indians several years earlier.

Enemies and Allies (page 23)

Jamestown Massacre: Powhatans vs. English

Pequot War: Pequots vs. English plus Mohicans and Narragansetts

King Philip's War: Wampanoags and Narragansetts vs. English

Pueblo Uprising: Pueblos and Apaches vs. Spanish

Tuscarora War: Yamasees and English vs. Tuscaroras

Yamasee War: Yamasees vs. English and Cherokees

French and Indian War: English and Iroquois vs. French plus Delawares and Hurons

Pontiac's War: Ottawas vs. British colonists

Close-up: The Fur Trade (page 24)

Environmental effects: Resource wiped out in some areas; fur-bearing animals were trapped out, moved elsewhere.

Social effects: Tribal groups relocated, away from agricultural lands and next to trading routes. Smaller groups formed larger alliances. Wars became more lethal. Some groups were almost exterminated.

Economic effects: Native Americans began accumulating trade goods, private property. Subsistence economy replaced by trade economy.

Time Line: Indian and Colonial Wars (page 25)

Jamestown Massacre, 1622

Pequot War, 1637

Second Jamestown attack, 1644

New Amsterdam becomes New York, 1664

King Philip's War (Metacom's War), 1675–76

Bacon's Rebellion, 1676

Pueblo Uprising, 1680

King William's War, 1689–97

New Mexico reconquest, 1692

Queen Anne's War, 1702–13

Deerfield Massacre, 1704

Tuscarora War, 1711–13

Yamasee War, 1715

King George's War, 1740–48

Fort Necessity battle, 1754

Ohio Valley attacks, 1754–55

French and Indian War, 1754–63

Fort Louisburg, Nova Scotia, falls, 1758

Fort Duquesne becomes Fort Pitt, 1758

Fort Niagara and Quebec fall, 1759

Montreal falls, 1760

Treaty of Paris, 1763

Pontiac's War, 1763

Additional Activity Suggestions

Students could do any of the following additional activities.

1. Tell the story in detail of one particular Indian group's experiences during the era of North American colonization. If you live in an area of the country that was colonized during this time, do research on a Native American group that lived locally. You could tell their story in the first person.

2. Make a list of Native American place names in your town, local area, region, county, or state. Or list Native American words that are used in the English language today.

3. Find quotes from Native Americans and Europeans that express their views of the land and land ownership. Use a poster or some other visual way to display and contrast these views.

4. Corn was perhaps the most valuable thing Native Americans introduced to Europeans. Make a poster showing the many uses of corn for North American people in the colonial era.

Unit 2 Assessment

Write a description, perhaps in diary or letter form, or as a newspaper or talk-show interview, of your experiences as a European settler captured by Indians. You lived with your captors for a while—perhaps for a long time. What did you learn about Native American culture? Did you want to return to European society? For background material for this activity, you could read some actual accounts of captivity.

Alternatively, describe the European person's capture and period of captivity from the point of view of one of the Native Americans involved. Why did you attack and capture the white people's settlement? Who were your allies? What are your plans for this white person? Did this person seem to have difficulty adapting to your culture?

Unit 3: The Rise of Individualism and the Seeds of Democracy

The Seeds of Democracy (page 34)

1. Self-government

2. Consent of the governed

3. Consent of the governed quotes:

   a. . . . full power and authority to rule themselves . . . by such a form of civil government as by voluntary consent of all, or the greater part of them, they shall find most suitable.

   b. That the common law or fundamental rights and privileges of West New Jersey are individually agreed upon by the proprietors and freeholders thereof to be the foundation of the government.

4. a. Inhabitants of the towns

   b. Freemen of the province

   c. Representative government

5. a. The signers agree to combine themselves "together into a civil body politic, for our better ordering and preservation," and plan to pass their own laws as they shall see fit that are best for their own colony—not that are best for the mother country.

   b. Again, the assembly is set up to have "free power to make laws" that are for the best interests of the colony—not Great Britain.

   c. Charter gives inhabitants "full power and authority to rule themselves" with whatever type of civil government they think best. More trouble for the king.

   d. Only laws agreed to by the general assembly shall be valid in the colony. The king's laws won't be accepted unless the assembly agrees to them.

6. a. Rule of law before anyone is punished or property taken away. No inhumane bodily punishment. Husbands can't whip their wives except in self-defense.

   b. Freedom of religious worship. Right to trial by jury of peers. Conviction only by testimony of at least two honorable witnesses. Freedom of speech in assembly. Right to elect justices and constables.

Colonial Rebellions (page 37)

Political Factors

Bacon's Rebellion—wealthy plantation owners controlling Virginia's government, ignoring western concerns.

Leisler's Rebellion—locals resenting English rule.

Paxton Boys' Uprising—westerners resenting easterners' control of assembly, ignoring western concerns.

Carolina Regulators—same as for Paxton Boys.

Economic Factors

Bacon's Rebellion—small growers couldn't compete with large plantation owners, who had much land; small owners got pushed out, couldn't make a living on worn-out tobacco soil.

Leisler's Rebellion—perhaps anger from trader's point of view about English restrictions on trade.

Paxton Boys' Uprising—westerners not as well off as prosperous easterners.

Carolina Regulators—poorer westerners pitted against wealthier coastal, low-country planters.

Social Factors

Bacon's Rebellion—wealthy plantation owners looking down on poorer western frontier dwellers, who resent the easterners' social pretensions and attitudes.

Leisler's Rebellion—the local militia leader resenting superior-acting English rulers.

Paxton Boys' Uprising—again, frontier dwellers resenting easterners looking down on them.

Carolina Regulators—big social difference between aristocratic Anglican-English coastal society and backcountry Scotch-Irish and other lower-class people.

Geographic Factors

Bacon's Rebellion, Paxton Boys' Uprising, Carolina Regulators—split between coastal plantation (large, wealthy planters) and back-country (subsistence frontier dwellers).

Leisler's Rebellion— geography not a factor (except that Leisler, an American colonist, rejects British rule).

Pattern is east vs. west; older settled area vs. frontier; higher-class society vs. lower-class working society; status quo vs. independent-minded people.

Can You Vote? Can You Be Elected? (page 39)

1. Yes; you are a freeman, inhabitant of the colony.

2. Yes; you are a freeman of the province.

3. Yes, if you're worth £50; all inhabitants over 21 and worth £50 can vote.

4. No; you don't profess a belief in Jesus Christ as Savior.

5. No; you don't belong to an approved church.

6. Yes; bound servants can vote—but if they don't, they don't have to pay a fine as freemen do.

7. Yes; you are an inhabitant.

8. No; you have to own 50 acres of land (or be worth at least £50 pounds, in which case you could vote).

9. No; you are not a free **man**.

10. No; you are not a freeholder or householder because you live in a rented room in a house you are not head of.

11. Vote: yes; you own 100 acres.

    Be elected: No; don't own at least 500 acres.

12. Vote 1740: yes; very unrestricted vote.

    Vote 1760: no; now you must own 100 acres of land.

Challenge Questions answers:

a. It becomes more restricted—more property and wealth requirements creep in.

b. Women, sometimes non-Christians, nonlandowners, poorer people, nonfreemen.

Time Line: Political Rights and Conflicts
(page 41)

Charters, Acts, Assemblies

House of Burgesses meets, 1619

Mayflower Compact, 1620

Charter of Maryland, 1634

Fundamental Orders of Connecticut, 1639

Massachusetts Body of Liberties, 1641

Patent of Providence Plantations, 1643

Maryland Toleration Act, 1649

New Netherland self-government, 1653

Fundamental Constitutions of Carolina, 1669–70

Fundamental Rights of West New Jersey, 1677

Pennsylvania Frame of Government, 1682

Pennsylvania Charter of Privileges, 1701

Delaware Assembly meets, 1703

Royal charter for Georgia, 1732

Ohio Company royal charter, 1749

Rebellions

Bacon's Rebellion, 1676

Leisler's Rebellion, 1689–91

Paxton Boys' Uprising, 1763

Carolina Regulators Rebellion, 1771

Events in England

Glorious Revolution, 1689

English Bill of Rights, 1689

Additional Activity Suggestions

Students could do any of the following additional activities.

1. With classmates, draw up a set of rules to govern your classroom. Each class member must be willing to sign an agreement to abide by all the rules.

2. Find out what the early rules for voting and holding public office were in your town or city. When were these rules expanded (or restricted)?

3. You are a colonial woman. Construct an argument about why you should be allowed to vote. Deliver your argument aloud to the governing body (all men) of your town or colony.

Unit 3 Assessment

Democracy planted its seeds in colonial North America. But no colony was governed as a democracy. Describe in specific detail the elements of democracy in colonial governments. Also explain what was not democratic about these governments.

Unit 4: Religious Diversity and Freedom

Religious Immigrants (page 45)

1. Pilgrims

   From: Holland, where they'd settled after leaving England
   To: Massachusetts, New England
   Why: To practice their faith without following Church of England rituals and practices

2. Anglicans

   From: England
   To: Virginia, Maryland, South Carolina
   Why: For economic and social, not religious, reasons. Their religious practice mirrored England's.

3. Puritans

   From: England
   To: Massachusetts, New England
   Why: To practice faith without Church of England rituals and practices

4. Huguenots

   From: France
   To: Coastal South Carolina, Philadelphia, New York
   Why: To escape persecution in Catholic France after Edict of Nantes was revoked in 1685

5. Dutch Reformed Church members

From: Netherlands
To: New Netherland (New York and vicinity)
Why: For social and economic reasons. Their Dutch Reformed Church was the same as in Netherlands.

6. Roman Catholics

   From: England; also from Spain to Spanish colonies
   To: Maryland, also Georgia; Spanish colonies—New Mexico, Florida
   Why: To escape persecution in England; to spread Catholicism in Spanish colonies, and to settle there for social and economic reasons

7. Quakers

   From: England
   To: Pennsylvania, New Jersey, Rhode Island
   Why: To escape persecution; went to colonies with religious toleration

8. Presbyterians

   From: Scotland, northern Ireland
   To: backcountry South and Pennsylvania
   Why: To escape what they thought was unfair rule by English Anglicans

9. Mennonites and Moravians

   From: Germany
   To: Pennsylvania
   Why: To escape persecution in Germany

10. Jews

    From: Spain, Portugal
    To: major port cities (New York/New Amsterdam, Rhode Island, Philadelphia), Georgia
    Why: To escape persecution, intolerance in Catholic countries

11. Lutherans

    From: Germany, Sweden
    To: Pennsylvania, Delaware
    Why: To practice their faith in peace

12. Protestantism and Judaism

13. Pacifism

Degrees of Religious Freedom (page 50)

1. Massachusetts

   Allowed: All Christian faiths except Catholicism

   Why: To be sure all religious practice in the colony was Christian (but only Puritan church members could participate in government)

2. Rhode Island

   Allowed: All religious practices, or none
   Why: As set up by Roger Williams, who was banished from Massachusetts by the Puritans because of his unorthodox beliefs

3. New Netherland

   Allowed: Privately, any religious belief; publicly, only the Dutch Reformed Church worship
   Why: Too difficult to allow only colonists who belonged to Dutch Reformed Church, but an attempt to control public worship and keep the church under the colony's control.

4. Pennsylvania

   Allowed: All religious beliefs, but not atheism—must believe in one God, the Creator
   Why: Colony established by William Penn, a Quaker, who wanted a haven from persecution

5. New Jersey

   Allowed: All religious practices
   Why: Colony established by Quakers, to provide a haven from persecution

6. Maryland

   Allowed: All Christian practices
   Why: Colony established by the Calverts, Roman Catholics, who wanted freedom of religious practice for Catholics as well as Protestants

7. Virginia

   Allowed: Church of England was the colony's official religion; other religions were not much interfered with
   Why: Leaders and landowners were mostly Anglican; need for settlers meant other religions had to be allowed

8. Carolinas

   Allowed: All religions, although Anglican church was the colony's official religion
   Why: Same as for Virginia; see box, "Why Allow for Freedom of Worship."

9. <u>New Haven</u>

   Allowed: To participate in government, only members of "approved churches," i.e., Puritan or other Congregational
   Why: Colony established as a community covenanted with God, conducted according to God's laws

10. <u>Georgia</u>

   Allowed: All religious faiths except Catholicism
   Why: A founding principle of colony's organizers

Questions:

1. No. Deviation from Puritan leaders' interpretation of God's rules and laws was not tolerated. Dissenters were banished.

2. In Puritan colonies, in early times, yes. Otherwise, no. Colonies needed settlers, so live and let live became the prevailing practice.

Living Like a Puritan (page 52)

1. Individual expression, opinion, action: Individuals are to mold their behavior to community standards, which are based on the laws of God. Individual expression is rebellion against God.

2. Role of magistrates: Receive their authority from God, so obedience to them is required. The laws they enforce are the laws of God, so people must obey them. Magistrates are chosen by church members, so they are godly men.

3. Role of ministers, religious leaders: They consult with magistrates in matters of religion and religious laws and rules of conduct. They also consult with magistrates in all important civil matters. They are powerful figures in the community and monitor behavior of people in all areas.

4. Role of the people in government: People who are covenanted with God—i.e., church members—choose their governors (magistrates, church leaders, etc.). They don't make laws; they live by the laws of God (as set out in the Bible and identified as such by their religious leaders).

5. Authority within family: Flows downward from husband, who is the family's ruler as Christ is the head of the church. Wives obey husbands in all things. Children obey both parents in all things.

The Dissenters (page 53)

1. They disagreed with their religious leaders, and publicly at that. They gathered followers who agreed that the ministers weren't necessarily correct. Williams said the magistrates had no right to enforce religious laws—a complete contradiction of the Puritan structure of society. Hutchinson said "saved" people didn't have to live by the Puritan laws, or even the laws of the colony.

2. They were dangerous. The Puritan leaders wanted no one in the colony who would challenge the Puritan code—to live by the rules of God set out by the community's leaders. Otherwise, the community would no longer be holy.

3. Separation of Church and State.

A Famous Sermon (page 56)

You will want to review proposed speeches to be sure they are appropriate for the classroom. You don't want a student delivering one of Adolf Hitler's harangues! Examples of appropriate choices would include Martin Luther King, Jr.'s "I Have a Dream" speech; an athletic coach trying to inspire a team to victory; a suffragist's speech; a general trying to rally troops; a prohibitionist denouncing the evils of alcohol; a muckraker exposing some corrupt practice or business.

Additional Activity Suggestions

Students could do any of the following additional activities.

1. In a small group, make a list of "meaningful" Puritan first names, like Charity and Prudence. Use library research and novels or films about colonial America and the Puritans for your sources. [Teacher note: These names could get very elaborate, like Truthshallprevaile, or seem startling today, like Freelove. Share these two names with students to encourage them to find more unusual names

of these types. See who can come up with the most names unduplicated by any other group.]

2. With classmates, act out scenes from *The Crucible*, Arthur Miller's drama about the Salem witch trials.

3. Choose a partner. One of you takes the part of a Quaker. The other is a Puritan. Then role-play a debate. The Puritan insists that the Quaker be whipped and banished from the colony—maybe even hanged. The Quaker explains why he or she must remain in the colony. Can either of you convince the other to change position?

4. As a class or a small group, discuss the validity of the quotations from Winthrop and Calvin in the student activities about the relationship between husbands and wives. Find other original source quotes on the same topic. How has this relationship changed in the course of U.S. history?

Unit 4 Assessment

Write a dialogue between two colonial people. One, like William Penn, is in favor of religious toleration. The other, like Cotton Mather, believes that only his church's practices should be allowed as public worship. Express their viewpoints.

Unit 5: Social and Cultural Life

Student Background Pages (page 58)

The quote from Increase Mather is from his tract titled "An Arrow Against Profane and Promiscuous Dancing." Some of the vocabulary may be difficult for some students. You could conduct a class exercise to paraphrase the quote, especially the sentence that reads, "The unchaste touches and gesticulations used by dancers have a palpable tendency to that which is evil."

Many source books, including *The Annals of America, Vol. 1*, have the complete alphabet verses from the *New England Primer*. Students might enjoy reading all of them instead of just the excerpt here.

Men's Work, Women's Work, Children's Work (page 60)

Children helped with almost all chores. Young boys helped with spinning and weaving and other "women's" work, along with the girls. Indicated here are chores that were mainly men's (and older boys') and mainly women's. Hoeing, weeding, and tending the kitchen garden was mostly children's work.

clearing land: men (older boys)	planting crops: men (older boys)
making butter: women	making cheese: women
making soap: women	plowing fields: men (older boys)
chopping up firewood: men (older boys)	making beer and cider: women
spinning yarn: women	creating clothing: women
butchering cattle: men (older boys)	harvesting crops: men
butchering chickens: women	hunting for wild game: men (older boys)
building and mending fences: men (older boys)	milking cows: men, women
washing clothing: women	hauling water: women
cooking meals: women	weaving wool into cloth: women
making iron tools: men	shearing sheep: men (older boys)
hoeing, weeding, tending the kitchen garden: children	dying fabric: women

Life in New England (Forefathers' Song) (page 61)

Have musically talented students set this to music. Have other students recite it aloud—individually or as a group, portions of it or all, from memory or by reading.

Colonial Houses (page 62)

"A large, elegant house . . ."—the southern plantation-style mansion

Region: the southern tidewater

"The houses were made of thin, small cedar shingles . . ."—New England saltbox

Region: New England

"Most of the houses in this part of the country . . ."—log cabin

Region: frontier areas, mostly in western backcountry

"This little hut was one of the wretchedest . . ."—frontier hut or slave cabin

Region: Southern slave plantations; poor areas of the frontier everywhere

Crime and Punishment (page 63)

1. f	10. n
2. a	11. d
3. k	12. l
4. h	13. m
5. g	14. e
6. i	15. c
7. p	16. q
8. b	17. o
9. j	

Time Line: Social and Cultural Life (page 64)

Education Laws:

Massachusetts Bay Colony school law, 1642

Plymouth Colony school law (a school for every town with at least 50 families), 1647

Connecticut school law (a school for every town with at least 50 families), 1673

Colleges are founded:

Harvard College, 1636

the College of William and Mary, 1693

the Collegiate School in New Haven (becomes Yale), 1701

the College of New Jersey (becomes Princeton), 1746

King's College (becomes Columbia), 1754

the College of Philadelphia (becomes the University of Pennsylvania), 1755

Rhode Island College (becomes Brown University), 1764

Queen's College (becomes Rutgers), 1766

Dartmouth College, 1769

Publications:

The New England Primer, c. 1688

John Smith's *A True Relation . . . of Virginia,* 1608

Poor Richard's Almanack, 1732

John Eliot's Bible in the Algonquian language, 1663

Religious and Cultural Events

the Great Awakening, 1730's–1740's

Jonathan Edwards's sermon "Sinners in the Hands of an Angry God," 1741

Science and Intellectual Life

Franklin invents the Franklin stove, 1740

Franklin conducts kite experiment with lightning and electricity, 1752

Rittenhouse builds an orrery, 1767

North American colonies' first modern hospital, in Philadelphia, 1755

Challenge Question answer: An orrery is an instrument that shows the relations among the bodies in the solar system.

Benjamin Franklin: An American Original
(page 65)

Paraphrasing will vary. Samples follow.

1. Praises acting, not talking about acting.

2. Criticizes drinking too much alcohol.

3. Praises hard, honest labor. Criticizes a gentleman's life of leisure.

4. Criticizes the competence of doctors and the way they collect a fee even when they're not responsible for the cure.

5. Praises thrift; criticizes being careless about small expenses.

6. Praises being skilled at a trade.

7. Tells people to be sure to pay attention to small faults.

8. Criticizes the way in which the least worthy people rise to the top positions in bad government, while worthier, weightier people remain at the bottom, the way heavy objects sink in water.

9. Praises people who stay away from involvement with other people's money or women.

10. Notes that wealth does not make a person content.

11. Criticizes people who stay too long with those they're visiting.

12. Criticizes being ashamed of being poor. Does not criticize being poor, though.

13. Praises valuing a person for personal qualities, not for social standing.

14. Praises learning from experience.

15. Notes that the gadgets and technology men accumulate are equivalent to the toys they had as youngsters.

16. Advises to practice compromise and acceptance after marriage.

17. Praises valuing people for what they do, not what their families have done.

18. Notes that a king is only a human being, like the rest of us; an expression of American disinclination to be in awe of royalty.

19. Criticizes abstract learning that doesn't prepare a person for real life.

20. Praises work.

21. Notes that kings can be unpredictable and worrisome to their advisors; another expression of American lack of awe of royalty.

22. Again, American lack of awe of royalty—princes often act childishly.

The new American character, on the whole, is independent, hardworking, egalitarian, thrifty, practical, down-to-earth, rational, definitely nonroyalist.

Additional Activity Suggestions

Students could do any of the following additional activities.

1. Read all of the alphabet verses of *The New England Primer*. Then make up a set of your own, for colonial New England but more lighthearted. Or make up a set of alphabet verses for another colonial region: *The Southern Primer, The Philadelphia Primer, The New York Primer, The Pennsylvania Primer,* etc.

2. Demonstrate to classmates some of the games colonial kids played. What games were children allowed to play in the strict Puritan society?

3. Compose a "Forefathers' Song" for other colonial regions.

4. Read some of Anne Bradstreet's poetry. Also, learn some details about her life. What do you find out from this about the life of women in colonial New England?

Unit 5 Assessment

The group activity "How They Lived" makes an effective assessment tool for this unit.

Unit 6: The Colonial Economy

Colonial Resources: Mapping (page 73)

beaver—New England, Canada

timber and lumber products—New England, New York

fish—New England

rum distilling—New England (especially Rhode Island)

shipbuilding—New England

tobacco—Virginia, Maryland, portions of North Carolina

grains, flour—Pennsylvania, middle colonies

rice—South Carolina

indigo—South Carolina

naval stores—Carolinas, Georgia, New York

iron—middle colonies

small manufacturing—middle colonies

small subsistence farming—New England, back-country of southern colonies

large farming—Pennsylvania

large plantations—southern colonies

small cash crops—middle colonies, some areas of New England

Colonial Resources: Exports and Imports (page 74)

Challenge Questions answers:

1. New England; it was a region of small subsistence farming or trade of natural resources. Few manufactured goods were produced here.

2. Virginia and Maryland; their economy was based on production of tobacco for export to England.

3. Yes; many more *exports* from England—earning England money—than *imports* from the Colonies, costing England money.

Mercantilism: Mapping (page 75)

1.

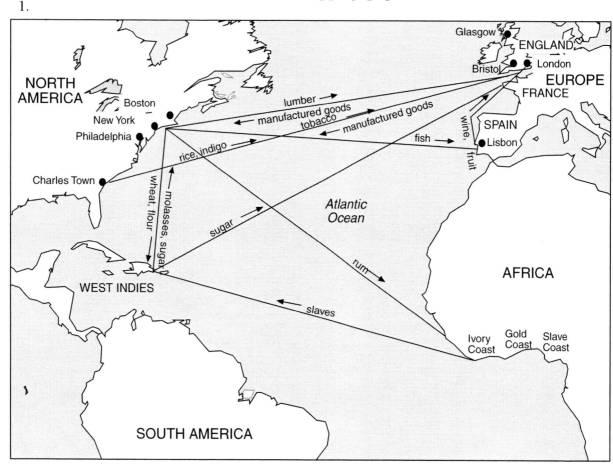

fish (from New England area to Portugal, southern Spain)	wine, fruit (from Portugal, southern Spain to London area)	manufactured goods (from England back to New England area)
rice, indigo (from Charles-town, S.C., area to London)	manufactured goods (reverse back to South Carolina)	
wheat, flour (from Philadel-phia to West Indies)	sugar (from West Indies to London)	manufactured goods (from London to Philadelphia)
rum (from New England to Ivory/Gold/Slave Coasts of Africa)	slaves (from West Africa coasts to West Indies, Caribbean islands)	molasses, sugar (from Carib-bean islands to New England)
tobacco (from Virginia, South Carolina ports to England)	manufactured goods (reverse back)	
lumber (from northern New England to England)	manufactured goods (reverse back)	

Economic Choices (page 76)

Students are free to choose what they want. Likely choices based on the geographic/economic situation follow.

1. tobacco farming

2. rum distilling, shipbuilding and shipping—triangular trade; fishing; ship crafts

3. trade; artisan and craft enterprises of all kinds; maritime trade and activities; get land and start farming outside the city

4. fur trade; timber products

5. shipping; social life services; rice, indigo planting

6. hunting; fur trapping; subsistence farming

Comparing Colonial Workers (page 78)

Indentured Servant

Terms of Work: Bound for a certain number of years, usually 4 to 7; in return, master must provide food, lodging, clothing, usually some education or training.

Why Come: For economic opportunity or because English legal authorities force them to (debtor, vagrant, poor person, orphan, etc.).

Advantages and Disadvantages: Will be free at end of service and will get clothing, tools, etc., maybe land, at end of service. But during service may be treated terribly by master and has no personal freedom—can't even have a romantic relationship with anyone.

Slave

Terms of Work: Lifelong servitude, no pay, no skill training, no rights

Why: Because of being captured, forced into slavery

Advantages and Disadvantages: No advantages. Lifetime as a slave, lifetime of hard labor, ripped from native country, home, family, etc.

Transported Convict

Terms: Maybe free on arrival in America, more likely signed to a term of service like an indentured servant

Why: Forced to come by English legal authorities

Advantages and Disadvantages: Escape death or long jail terms in England, with good prospects for economic advancement after service term ends; suffer unpleasant conditions as a bound servant

Free Immigrant/Native Colonist:

Terms: Free to do whatever

Why: Came for economic opportunities, opportunities to practice religious faith freely, or for adventure; born here

Advantages and Disadvantages: Live freely, do what you want, make your own fortune

Extra Challenge answer: Indentured servants bound themselves out ahead of time, before they got on the ship. Redemptioners couldn't pay for their passage; they struck a deal with the ship's captain that upon arrival they would sell their services to a master who would pay for their passage. Redemptioners were supposed to be able to shop around and choose the best situation for themselves once they got to the colonies. In practice, they often couldn't even leave the ship and had to accept whatever service contracts potential masters who boarded the ship once it was in the harbor offered to them.

The Navigation Acts and You (page 80)

1. You can ship your tobacco only to ports that are part of the British Empire.

2. You have lots of business; colonial imports and exports have to be carried either in colonial or in British ships, and shipbuilding is much more economical in the colonies than in England because the wood needed for ship-building is abundant in Maine.

3. You're fine; the Navigation Acts allow you to ship wheat and flour anywhere in the world.

4. You're okay at first, but the later Acts say you have to ship rice only within the British Empire.

5. You can ship fish anywhere; the Acts don't apply to you.

6. The Act of 1660 says you can ship indigo only within the British Empire.

7. Your wine has to be shipped from France to England, be unloaded there, and then reloaded before being shipped to you—you pay for all this extra shipping and handling.

8. The later Acts say you can't import molasses from West Indies colonies that aren't British (but you probably do anyway, ignoring the law).

Additional Activity Suggestions

Students could do any of the following additional activities.

1. Read some historical fiction to understand better the hardships of being an indentured servant. Examples: *Calico Bush*, by Rachel Field, and *Master Entrick*, by Michael Mott. Use what you read to make a chart showing the advantages and disadvantages of being an indentured servant.

2. Discuss with classmates the accuracy of this quote by a contemporary New Yorker about people in the colonies in the 1700's: "The only principle of life propagated among the young people is to get money, and men are only esteemed according to what they are worth, that is, the money they are possessed of." Would this apply to all colonies and areas within the colonies?

3. Add resource symbols to your map for the West Indies and South America.

Unit 6 Assessment

You could assess students' learning in either of these ways.

1. Compare the economics of the following: family farming in New England, larger-scale farming in Pennsylvania, plantation agriculture in the southern tidewater/Chesapeake region, and yeoman farming in the southern back country.

2. Describe in detail the business activities and home life of a Boston shipping merchant or a Philadelphia artisan.

Unit 7: The Rise of Slavery

Mapping the Slave Trade (page 85)

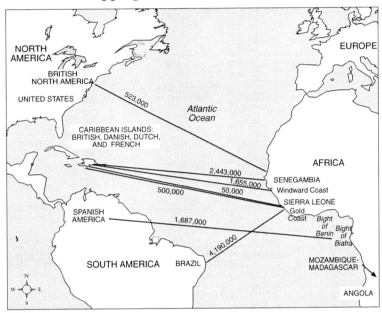

3. a. Brazil (or Caribbean as a whole—
        4,648,000)

    b. 523,000

    c. 10,525,000

4. Because Brazil was a Portuguese colony.

Reading the Slave Trade Graph (page 87)

1. Portugal

2. Great Britain

3. Netherlands, United States

4. 350,000

5. 1751–1800

6. 1701–1810—1,900,000

    1811–1870—1,450,000

7. 6 million

8. Portugal

The other countries outlawed the slave trade.

African-American Culture (page 92)

1. **religion:** Added African spirituality to create
   an emotionally expressive form of Christianity; identified with Bible stories of the Jews in
   slavery in Egypt and their eventual freedom;
   meeting for religious purposes was permitted
   (slave gatherings were otherwise mostly
   prohibited), which gave African slaves the
   chance to create fellowship.

2. **music:** Melded originally created English
   verses with African musical tones, rhythms,
   and forms—especially call-and-response—
   to create a new African-American musical
   form, the spiritual; fashioned musical instru-
   ments similar to those they had used in Africa.

3. **family structure:** Slaves married in the European manner where allowed to do so, even
   though the unions were not legally recog-
   nized, and added some African customs like
   jumping the broomstick; took in those whose
   families had been sold away, creating
   extended family units; worked poorly when
   the family was broken up, thus discouraging
   owners from selling families apart (although
   this still happened often enough).

4. **literacy (reading and writing):** Taught each
   other secretly, by candlelight at night or
   hidden in the woods; passed down personal/
   family history orally, in the African tradition.

5. **language:** Spoke English, but kept some African words, like *banjo, yam, okra;* developed a black dialect.

Extra Challenge answers:

a. crops: rice-planting and cultivation techniques; yams

b. animal raising: better techniques for herding cattle

c. fishing: improved nets

Time Line: Slavery (page 93)

1619   A Dutch ship brings 20 blacks to Jamestown, Virginia

1621   Dutch West Indies Company founded

1620's–1630's Dutch take over Portuguese slave trading

1662   Virginia law: children born of a slave woman are slaves; African slaves are "perpetual servants" [**Note:** A similar law was passed in Maryland, 1664.]

1663   Plot to rebel discovered among black slaves and white indentured servants in Virginia

1667   Virginia law: slaves who are baptized as Christians remain slaves

1669   Slave revolt in Jamaica

1669   Virginia law: a master who kills a slave he is punishing for resistance of any kind faces no legal penalty

1687   Virginia slave plot exposed; leaders executed

1712   New York City slave revolt; about 25 blacks, some whites killed

1730–40 Almost yearly, slave revolts in Jamaica

1731   Guianas revolt (approximately 18 from this date to end of slavery)

1739   Stono, South Carolina, rebellion; about 100 slaves defeated in hard battle with militia, Indians

1740–41 New York plot foiled; over 100 accused

1740   Slave plot to capture Annapolis, Maryland

1751   South Carolina law: death penalty to slaves who try to poison whites

1760   Tacky's rebellion in Jamaica, about 1,000 slaves

Additional Activity Suggestions

Students could do any of the following additional activities.

1. Sing "O, Wasn't That a Wide River," the spiritual in the Student Background Pages (or another similar song) with classmates in a call-and-response style. Feel the rhythm. Do you see how this could be a good accompaniment to group field work?

2. Write a biography of Abd al-Rahman Ibrahima, an African prince captured and sold into slavery in the Americas who fought for his freedom up to the highest levels of American government.

3. Create pie charts or other graphs showing the percentage of white and black populations in various colonies over time in the 1600's and 1700's. You can find the raw data in *Historical Statistics of the United States, Colonial Times to 1970—Part 2* (U.S. Department of Commerce, Bureau of the Census). The raw data are set up in a percentage table in the appendix to *American Slavery 1619–1877*, by Peter Kolchin (New York: Hill and Wang, 1993).

4. Read some eyewitness accounts of the slave trade. Examples: Charles Ball, *A Narrative of the Life and Adventures of Charles Ball, A Black Man.* George Francis Dow, *Slave Ships and Slaving.* Theophile Conneau, *A Slaver's Log Book: Twenty Years' Residence in Africa.* Olaudah Equiano, *The Interesting Narrative of the Life of Olaudah Equiano or Gustavus Vasa, Written by Himself.*

Unit 7 Assessment

You are an African brought to the Americas as a slave. Describe your experience: the capture, the trek to the coast, the voyage aboard ship to the Americas, your sale to a slave owner, your new life in America, your relations with fellow slaves and whites, the ways in which you put elements of your African culture into the new life that is forced on you. Be sure to tell how you feel about what's happening to you.

ADDITIONAL RESOURCES

Historical Fiction for Students

Avi. *Encounter at Easton* (indentured servants escape).

Berry, James. *Ajeemah and His Son* (Africans sold into slavery).

Bulla, Clyde Robert. *John Billington, Friend of Squanto* (Plymouth).

Clapp, Patricia. *Constance: A Story of Early Plymouth*.

Farber, Norma. *Mercy Short* (1600's Massachusetts).

Field, Rachel. *Calico Bush* (indentured servitude).

Latham, Jean. *This Dear-Bought Land* (John Smith and Jamestown).

Miller, Arthur. *The Crucible* (classic drama about the Salem witch craze).

Mott, Michael. *Master Entrick* (indentured servitude).

O'Dell, Scott. *The Serpent Never Sleeps: A Novel of Jamestown and Pocahontas*.

Speare, Elizabeth. *Calico Captive* (New England colonists captured by Native Americans).

_____. *Sign of the Beaver* (white boy and Native Americans in frontier Maine).

_____. *The Witch of Blackbird Pond* (life in 1600's New England).

Ziner, Fennie. *Squanto* (Plymouth).

Nonfiction for Students

Primary Sources

Bradford, William. *Of Plymouth Plantation*.

Conneau, Theophile. *A Slaver's Log Book: Twenty Years' Residence in Africa*.

Franklin, Benjamin. *Autobiography* and *Poor Richard's Almanack*.

Smith, John. *The General History of Virginia*.

Vasa, Gustavus. *The Interesting Narrative of the Life of Olaudah Equiano or Gustavus Vasa, Written by Himself*.

Winthrop, John. *History of New England*.

Reference Books

Alford, Terry. *Prince Among Slaves*.

Almanacs of American Life, Book 2: Colonial America, 1492–1763.

Downey, Matthew, ed. *America's Children: Voices from the Past*.

Fritz, Jean. *The Double Life of Pocahontas* (Jamestown).

_____. *Who's That Stepping on Plymouth Rock?*

McGovern, Ann. *If You Lived in Colonial Times*.

McKay, David. *How the Colonists Lived*.

Wright, Louis B. *Everyday Life in Colonial America*.

Collections of Primary Source Documents: Print

The Annals of America, Vol. 1. Chicago: Encylopedia Brittanica, 1968.

Commager, Henry Steele, ed. *Documents of American History,* 9th ed. (2 vols.). Englewood Cliffs, NJ: Prentice-Hall, 1973.

Craven, Avery, Walter Johnson, and F. Roger Dunn. *A Documentary History of the American People.* Boston: Ginn and Company, 1951.

Hart, Albert Bushnell. *American History as Told by Contemporaries* (5 volumes). New York: The Macmillan Company, 1901.

Historical Abstracts of the United States. Washington, DC: U.S. Department of Commerce, Bureau of the Census, 1975.

MacDonald, William, ed. *Select Charters and Other Documents Illustrative of American History 1606–1775.* New York: The Macmillan Company, 1899.

CD-ROM

America Adventure. Knowledge Adventure (also available as a DOS floppy disk).

American Indian 2.0. Facts On File.

American Journey—History in Your Hands: The African-American Experience. Research Publications.

American Journey—History in Your Hands: Women in America. Research Publications.

CD Sourcebook of American History. InfoBases.

500 Nations. Microsoft.

Landmark Documents in American History. Facts on File (dwarfs the print collections).

World Wide Web/Internet

Sites with Numerous Links to U.S. History Sources:

Government/Social Studies Sources (includes listings of Library of Congress exhibits, historical documents from Project Gutenburg, other social studies Web sites):
http://www.nwoca.ohio.gov/www/gov.html

History/Social Studies Web Site for K–12 Teachers (includes site map, What's New Archive, sources arranged by category):
http://www.execpc.com/~dboals/boals.html

Library of Congress home page (includes American Memory historical collections):
http://lcweb.loc.gov

Kathy Schrock's site (a Cape Cod teacher's excellent list of resources):
http://www.capecod.net/schrockguide

U.S. Historic Documents (primary documents in full text):
http://www.ukans.edu/carrie/docs/amdocs_index.html

GLOSSARY

almanac—a publication that gives weather information and predictions, plus a lot of other miscellaneous information.

charter—a constitution, or a written document setting up a colony.

colony—a territory that is tied to a parent state that controls it.

Columbian Exchange—the mutual impact European and Native American cultures had on each other.

dissenter—person who differs from the established beliefs of a religious group.

emigrate—to leave your native country for life in a different country.

enumerated products—items made in the British American colonies that were "enumerated," or named/listed, and thus could only be traded with the British Empire.

exports—goods sent out of a country or colony to another country or colony.

immigrate—to come into a country you are not a native of, intending to live there permanently.

imports—goods shipped into a country or colony from another country or colony.

indentured servant—person who sold himself or herself to a master for a given number of years; in return, the master paid for the servant's trip to America and living expenses.

mercantilism—government control of the national economy, stressing a favorable balance of trade—i.e., more exports than imports.

the Middle Passage—the slave ships' journey from Africa across the Atlantic Ocean to the Americas.

navigation—the method of getting ships from place to place.

ordinance—law.

Pilgrims—Protestants who separated from the "corrupt" Church of England and settled at Plymouth, Massachusetts, in 1620.

Puritans—members of a Protestant offshoot of the Church of England who practiced a "purified" form of the Anglican faith.

representative government—form of government in which voters choose people to represent (act for) them in a legislature (law-making body).

rights of Englishmen—liberties for all free English persons that the king (or queen) or Parliament couldn't take away.

triangular trade—three-way trade among New England, Africa, and the West Indies.

Share Your Bright Ideas with Us!

We want to hear from you! Your valuable comments and suggestions will help us meet your current and future classroom needs.

Your name_____Date_____

School name_____Phone_____

School address_____

Grade level taught_____Subject area(s) taught_____Average class size_____

Where did you purchase this publication?_____

Was your salesperson knowledgeable about this product?   Yes_____   No_____

What monies were used to purchase this product?

____School supplemental budget   ____Federal/state funding   ____Personal

Please "grade" this Walch publication according to the following criteria:

Quality of service you received when purchasing ....A   B   C   D   F
Ease of use..A   B   C   D   F
Quality of content..A   B   C   D   F
Page layout ....A   B   C   D   F
Organization of material ....A   B   C   D   F
Suitability for grade level ....A   B   C   D   F
Instructional value...A   B   C   D   F

COMMENTS:_____

_____

What specific supplemental materials would help you meet your current—or future—instructional needs?

_____

Have you used other Walch publications? If so, which ones?_____

May we use your comments in upcoming communications?   ____Yes   ____No

Please **FAX** this completed form to **207-772-3105**, or mail it to:

   Product Development, J.Weston Walch, Publisher, P.O. Box 658, Portland, ME 04104-0658

We will send you a **FREE GIFT** as our way of thanking you for your feedback. **THANK YOU!**